当代国际商务文化阅读丛书

Readings for Modern International Business Culture

伊斯特林悖论

——『感悟财富』篇

The Easterlin Paradox

Comprehension of Wealth

【英汉对照】

吴斐 编著

武汉大学出版社
WUHAN UNIVERSITY PRESS

图书在版编目(CIP)数据

伊斯特林悖论:“感悟财富”篇:英汉对照/吴斐编著.—武汉:武汉大学出版社,2016.5

当代国际商务文化阅读丛书

书名原文:The Easterlin Paradox:Comprehension of Wealth

ISBN 978-7-307-13993-0

Ⅰ.伊…　Ⅱ.吴…　Ⅲ.经济学—英、汉　Ⅳ.F0

中国版本图书馆 CIP 数据核字(2014)第 181961 号

责任编辑:郭园园　金　军　　责任校对:鄢春梅　　版式设计:韩闻锦

出版发行:**武汉大学出版社**　(430072　武昌　珞珈山)

(电子邮件:cbs22@whu.edu.cn 网址:www.wdp.com.cn)

印刷:武汉中远印务有限公司

开本:880×1230　1/32　印张:10.125　字数:221 千字

版次:2016 年 5 月第 1 版　　2016 年 5 月第 1 次印刷

ISBN 978-7-307-13993-0　　定价:28.00 元

前 言

人类社会进入21世纪后，国家间的商务往来更加频繁，商务交际手段随着互联网的诞生和电子信息的进步日新月异，国际化企业的文化和理念千差万别，商务话题的表达和沟通能力无疑是人们所遇到的最大障碍。在我们熟知的生活英语、学术英语之外，商务英语不仅是我国目前从事或即将从事涉外商务人员英语实际应用能力不可多得的辅助工具，更是商务工作人员在这个国际化的高科技时代商务竞争能力、外贸业务素质和英语水平的重要体现。《当代国际商务文化阅读》（英汉对照）丛书以从事国际商务活动所必需的语言技能为经，以各种商务活动的具体情景做纬，将商务精神和商务元素巧妙融合，展示时尚而又经典的商务文化世界流行风，为广大读者提供一套语言规范、内容新颖、涉及面广、趣味性强、具有实用价值、富于时代精神的读物，既注意解决人们在国际商务环境中遇到不熟悉的专业词汇无法与外国合作者就工作问题交流沟通的难题，又着力解决人们学外语单纯地学语言而缺乏商务专业知识的弊端。

《当代国际商务文化阅读》（英汉对照）丛书由10个单行本组成：《拥抱新欢亚马逊（Embracing Amazon Service）——电子商务篇

（E-commerce）》、《华尔街梦魇（Nightmare on Wall Street）——商界风云篇（The Business Circles)》、《路易斯·波森的朋克摇滚（The Punk Rock of Louis Posen）——商界精英篇（Business Elites）》、《希波克拉底誓言（Hippocratic Oath）——商务交际篇（Business Communication）》、《强烈的第一印象（A Powerful First Impression）——商务礼仪篇（Business Etiquette）》、《企业帝国继承权之争（Corporate Empires' Grappling with Succession）——商务文化篇（Business Culture）》、《紫色血液（The Purple Blood）——商务心理篇（Business Psychology）》、《多米诺骨牌效应（The Domino Effects）——商务知识篇（Business Knowledge）》、《公开的赌注（Public Stakes）——商务演讲篇（Business Speeches）》、《伊斯特林悖论（The Easterlin Paradox）——感悟财富篇（Comprehension of Wealth）》。这套丛书的编写旨在帮助读者在国际商务环境下，能够读懂英文的商务信息和商务新闻，并能对某一商务话题的知识有全面透彻的了解，领悟当代时尚商务文化成长的环境和思维方式，提高在全球化高科技时代的商务竞争能力、外贸业务素质和英语交际水平。丛书中的阅读材料力求做到题材广泛、内容精辟、语言规范，并遵循趣味性、知识性和时效性原则，培养读者在商务环境下的英语竞争能力和综合应用能力。丛书融时代性与经典性为一体，内容经得起时间考验，文字经得起反复咀嚼，保证其可读性。读者在阅读过程中接收大量的语言输入，为合理组织和娴熟运用英语语言表达自己的思想打下牢固的基础。丛书的单行本包括以一个主题为中心的 30 篇文章，每篇文章包括题记、英语原文、汉语译文、生词脚注和知识链接。“题记”用丰富生动的语言点评文章的精髓，对文章的内容起到提炼和画龙点睛的作用。"英语原文"主要摘自当代国际主流报纸杂志，具有语言规范、内容新颖、涉及面广、趣味性和时代感等特点。"汉语译文"力求准确流畅，既关注译文的文化语境及其内涵，也重视译文的外延和现当代标志性语言符号。"生词脚注"的难度把握在大学英语六级和研究生英语词汇程度，以帮助读者及时扫清阅读障碍。"知识链接"根据文章内容，或精解一个专业术语，或阐释一种新的商务理念，或介绍叱咤商界的企业或公司，以帮助读者培养游弋商海、运筹帷幄的能力，具备洞悉中西文化的国际视野。

《伊斯特林悖论》(The Easterlin Paradox)——"感悟财富"篇(Comprehension of Wealth)为读者展示了伊斯特林悖论、对财富的重新定义、资产的健康平衡、财富的宇宙意识、投资秘诀和理财概念、财富与自由、金钱与快乐、自制百万富翁的秘密、西方的精神贫乏与东方的物质贫困，以及"盖茨比"指南等极具诱惑、又发人深省的财富百态。财富从远古的甲骨和贝壳向我们走来，伴随着人类文明的进步和成长，在奢华与贫穷的两级中转换，品尝着人间的喜怒哀乐。当现代快乐经济学研究得出"钱不能买到幸福"的结论时，人类追逐财富、寻找幸福的奋斗又增添了新的含义。"伊斯特林悖论"启示我们，幸福并不取决于绝对收入，而取决于相对收入；人们感到悲伤，不是因为贫穷，而是由于他们发现自己处于某个特定群体的底层。今天的世界，人们正在经历着国民的快乐与幸福感不再随着收入增长而增长的现实。人们开始重新定义财富的认知价值观，"现有富裕派"宁愿付更多的佣金维持财富，教育孩子承担财政责任和慈善施舍；而"新晋富裕派"则崇尚创造财富而不是守住财富，鼓励人们游戏于投资和理财领域，把握住赚取财富的大好时机。人们开始寻找自制百万富翁的秘密，培养自己积极的工作态度、充满梦想的生活热情和持之以恒的心灵意志。人们开始拓展财富与自由的生态环境，将手中的金钱视作保持自由的一种工具。人们开始学习投资秘诀和理财概念，面对财富的机会长袖善舞、保持一份淡定和感激。人们开始理解资产的健康平衡和财富的宇宙意识，借助推动力、企业家身份、成就感和社交创造来保持一种幸福平衡。人们开始探讨西方的精神贫乏与东方的物质贫困，珍惜财富的精神基础和人性化的原则。

财富在绝望中诞生，在半信半疑中成长，在憧憬中成熟，在希望中毁灭。让我们伴随财富从远古带来渴望、在现代文明中创造的幸福和快乐、留给未来的憧憬和追逐，感悟财富在感恩、高贵、文明、和谐的人类文化长河中优雅而质朴的流动，享受世界流行文化创造的快乐、荣誉、价值和成就感！

作　者

2016年1月

目　录

目　录

目 录

题　记

现代经济学构建于“财富增加将导致福利或幸福增加”的核心命题之上。然而，令人迷惑的是：为什么更多的财富并没有带来更大的幸福？“伊斯特林悖论”启示我们，幸福并不取决于绝对收入，而取决于相对收入；人们感到悲伤，不是因为贫穷，而是由于他们发现自己处于某个特定群体的底层。日本人在“二战”后财富急剧增加，快乐感却明显下降；美国人的满足感没有提高的重要原因是大多数工人的小时工资近期没有大幅上升。当幸福的密码在拥有 iPod 和 iPad 之间转换时，人们其实正在以各种方式提醒自己，幸福实际上是一种追求、一种理想、一种境界。

The Easterlin Paradox

In the aftermath[①] of World War II, the Japanese economy went through one of the greatest booms the world has ever known. The economy's output per person grew more than sevenfold. Japan, in just a few decades, remade itself from a war-torn country into one of the richest nations on earth. Yet, strangely, Japanese citizens didn't seem to become any more satisfied with their lives. According to one poll, the percentage of people who gave the most positive possible answer about their life satisfaction actually fell. They were richer but apparently no happier. This contrast became the most famous example of a theory known as the Easterlin paradox. Richard Easterlin, an economist at the University of Pennsylvania, published a study in which he argued that economic growth didn't necessarily lead to more satisfaction.

People in poor countries, not surprisingly, did become happier once they could afford basic necessities. But beyond that, further gains simply seemed to reset the bar. To put it in today's terms, owning an iPod doesn't

---

① aftermath[ˈɑːftəmæθ] *n.* 不幸事件之后果，余波

伊斯特林悖论

"二战"后，日本经济经历了世上史无前例的繁荣。国民经济人均产出增长七倍多。日本在短短几十年内从一个饱受战争摧残的国家一跃发展成为世界上最富有的国家之一。但奇怪的是，日本国民看起来对生活不太满意。根据一项民意调查，日本人对生活满意度给出最积极、可能答案的比例确实有所下降。虽然他们更富有了，却明显缺乏更加快乐的感觉。这种反差成为伊斯特林悖论这种理论最有名的例子。宾夕法尼亚大学经济学家理查德·伊斯特林发表了一项研究，指出经济增长并不一定导致更高的满意度。

毫无疑问，生活在贫困国家的人一旦能够支付日常必需品就会变得更加快乐。但是除此之外，财富的进一步增加似乎只是重置了标准。以现今的话来说，拥有 iPod 并不一定让你感到快乐，因为你更想要 iPad。伊斯特林先生写道，相对收入，即相对于周围其他人的收入，你赚了多少远比绝对收入重要。此悖论很快成为社会科学的经典，被学术期刊和大众媒体引用。它演进成为一种近乎精神层

make you happier, because you then want an iPad. Relative income — how much you make compared with others around you — mattered far more than absolute income, Mr. Easterlin wrote. The paradox quickly became a social science classic, cited in academic journals and the popular media. It tapped into a near-spiritual human instinct to believe that money can't buy happiness. As a headline in The Financial Times said, "The Hippies Were Right All Along About Happiness." But now the Easterlin paradox is under attack.

At the Brookings Institution in Washington, two young economists — from the University of Pennsylvania, as it happens — presented a rebuttal① of the paradox. Their paper has quickly captured the attention of top economists around the world. It has also led to a spirited response from Mr. Easterlin. In the paper, Betsey Stevenson and Justin Wolfers argue that money indeed tends to bring happiness, even if it doesn't guarantee it. They point out that in the years since Mr. Easterlin published his paper, an explosion of public opinion surveys has allowed for a better look at the question. "The central message," Ms. Stevenson said, "is that income does matter." According to Gallup polls done around the world, life satisfaction is highest in the richest countries. The residents of these countries seem to understand that they have it pretty good, whether or not they own an iPad. If anything, Ms. Stevenson and Mr. Wolfers say, absolute income seems to matter more than relative income. In the United

① rebuttal[riˈbʌtəl] *n.* 反驳,反证

面的人类天性，认为金钱不能买到幸福。就像《金融时报》的头条标题："嬉皮士对幸福的理解一直都是正确的。"但是现在，伊斯特林悖论遭到抨击。

两位来自宾夕法尼亚大学的青年经济学家就在华盛顿布鲁金斯研究所对伊斯特林悖论提出了反驳。他们的报告很快吸引了世界顶级经济学家的关注。这份报告也引起了伊斯特林先生的积极反应。贝齐·史蒂文森和贾斯廷·沃尔弗斯在报告中提出，金钱确实有可能带来幸福，即使它不能保证幸福。他们指出，自伊斯特林先生发表他的文章以来，大规模的民意调查已经考虑采用更佳方式来看待这个问题。史蒂文森女士声称："核心信息是，收入确实至关重要。"根据世界范围内的盖洛普民意测验，富裕国家的人们生活满意度最高。无论有没有 iPad，这些国家的居民似乎认为他们的生活相当不错。史蒂文森女士和沃尔弗斯先生指出，如果有区别的话，绝对收入似乎比相对收入更重要。根据近期的盖洛普民意测验，年收入至少 25 万美元的美国家庭中大约有 90% 人称自己"非常幸福"。在年收入低于 3 万美元的家庭中，只有 42% 的人们给出相同的答案。但是，国际调查数据显示，年收入在 3 万美元以下的人群不太会感到幸福，即使他们生活在较贫穷的国家里。

即使是日本的异常也并不像它一开始看起来那样。史蒂文森女

States, about 90 percent of people in households making at least $ 250,000 a year called themselves "very happy" in a recent Gallup Poll. In households with income below $ 30,000, only 42 percent of people gave that answer. But the international polling data suggests that the under- $ 30,000 crowd might not be happier if they lived in a poorer country.

Even the Japanese anomaly① isn't quite what it first seems to be. Ms. Stevenson and Mr. Wolfers dug into those old government surveys and discovered that the question had changed over the years. In the early years, the most positive answer the pollsters offered was, "Although I am not innumerably② satisfied, I am generally satisfied with life now." Can you imagine an American poll offering that option? Then, the most positive answer became simply, "Completely satisfied." It is no wonder that the percentage of people giving this answer fell. When you look only at the years in which the question remained the same, the share of people calling themselves "satisfied" or "completely satisfied" did rise.

To put the new research into context, Someone called Daniel Kahneman, a Princeton psychologist who shared the 2002 Nobel Prize in economics. He has spent his career skewering③ economists for their belief that money is everything and has himself written about the "aspiration

---

① anomaly[əˈnɔməli] *n.* 异常,反常

② innumerably[iˈnjuːmərəbli] *ad.* 数不清地,无数地

③ skewer[ˈskjuə] *v.* 讽刺

士和沃尔弗斯先生仔细研究了前政府的调查报告，发现了问题的变化。民调专家在早期给出的最积极的答案是“虽然我有很多不满，但是总体来说，对现在生活感到满足”。但后来，最积极的答案变得简单明了：“完全满意。”所以，给出这种答案的人数百分比下降就不足为奇了。当你只关注问题保持不变的年份时，声称自己“满意”或“完全满意”的人数比例就会上升。

为了把这项新研究纳入轨道，有人打电话咨询了丹尼尔·卡恩曼，他是普林斯顿大学心理学教授、2002年诺贝尔经济学奖获奖者之一。他在职业生涯中一直在讽刺经济学家们提出的金钱万能的观点，并亲自撰写了伊斯特林悖论的核心部分——“激情跑步机”。但是卡恩曼先生说，他发现史蒂文森-沃尔弗斯报告“颇为引人注目。提供了大量越来越多的伊斯特林悖论有可能不存在的证据”。然后，又有人给现任南加利福尼亚大学教授的伊斯特林先生打了电话，他也收到了史蒂文森女士和沃尔弗斯先生报告的副本。他赞同更富有的国家的人们生活满意度更高的观点。但是，他也质疑由财富导致的满意度。他认为结果可以反过来说明，人们对调查问卷的回答方式存在文化差异。他接着说，如果满意度明显随着各国越来越富有而相应提高，他会更加信服。有些国家情况确实如此。但在其他一些国家，特别是美国和中国，却并非如此。他声称：“每

treadmill[①]" at the heart of the Easterlin paradox. Yet Mr. Kahneman said he found the Stevenson-Wolfers paper to be "quite compelling. There is just a vast amount of accumulating evidence that the Easterlin paradox may not exist." Others then called Mr. Easterlin, who's now at the University of Southern California and who had received a copy of the paper from Ms. Stevenson and Mr. Wolfers. He agreed that people in richer countries are more satisfied. But he's skeptical that their wealth is causing their satisfaction. The results could instead reflect cultural differences in how people respond to poll questions, he said. He would be more persuaded, he continued, if satisfaction had clearly risen in individual countries as they grew richer. In some, it has. But in others — notably the United States and China — it has not. "Everybody wants to show the Easterlin paradox doesn't hold up," he claimed. "And I'm perfectly willing to believe it doesn't hold up. But I'd like to see an informed analysis that shows that." He said he liked Ms. Stevenson and Mr. Wolfers personally, but he thought they had put out "a very rough draft without sufficient evidence." They, in turn, acknowledge that the data on individual countries over time is messy. But they note that satisfaction has risen in 8 of the 10 European countries. It has also risen in Japan. And a big reason it may not have risen in the United States is that the hourly pay of most workers has not grown much recently. "The time-series evidence is fragile," Mr. Wolfers said. "But it's more consistent with our story

---

① treadmill[ˈtredmil] *n.* 跑步机

个人都想证明，伊斯特林悖论是站不住脚的。我也完全心甘情愿地希望它站不住脚。但是，我想看到一份论据充足的分析报告来证明此事。”他说他个人非常欣赏史蒂文森女士和沃尔弗斯先生，但是他认为，他们提出的是“一份缺乏充分证据、非常粗糙的稿件”。史蒂文森和沃尔弗斯接着也承认，各国随时间推移的数据杂乱无章。但是他们指出，欧洲10国中有8个国家的满意度已经提高。日本的满意度也已经上升。美国人的满足感没有增加的重要原因是大多数工人的小时工资近期没有大幅上升。沃尔弗斯先生说:“时间序列证据很脆弱。但比起伊斯特林的报告，它与我们的结论更一致。”

那么，这些对我们来说意味着什么呢？就经济增长本身来说，确实不足以保证人们的福利——这就是伊斯特林对经济的伟大贡献。例如，这个国家的一些重大的卫生保健问题，如心脏疾病基本治疗的水平低下并不是因为资源匮乏。近期的研究发现，让人们感到最快乐的事，如短距离上下班、与朋友共度的时光，这些都与高收入毫无牵连。但是，如果把这个问题看得过重也是一种误解。事实是，经济增长并不只是以表层的物资形式使国家更富裕。经济增长也可以投资科学研究，为人类创造更长久、更健康的生命。它可以让人们去旅行，探望多年未见的亲戚，或者参观从未旅游过的

than his." So where does all this leave us?

Economic growth, by itself, certainly isn't enough to guarantee people's well-being — which is Mr. Easterlin's great contribution to economics. In this country, for instance, some big health care problems, like poor basic treatment of heart disease, don't stem from a lack of sufficient resources. Recent research has also found that some of the things that make people happiest — short commutes, time spent with friends — have little to do with higher incomes. But it would be a mistake to take this argument too far. The fact remains that economic growth doesn't just make countries richer in superficially materialistic ways. Economic growth can also pay for investments in scientific research that lead to longer, healthier lives. It can allow trips to see relatives not seen in years or places never visited. When you're richer, you can decide to work less — and spend more time with your friends.

Affluence is a pretty good deal. The people of the world seem to agree. At a time when the American economy seems to have fallen into recession and most families, incomes have been stagnant① for almost a decade, it's good to be reminded of why we should care.

(1,111 words)

---

① stagnant[ˈstægnənt] *a.* 不流动的,不景气的

景点。当你更加富有的时候，可以选择少干点工作——花更多的时间与朋友在一起。

富裕的物质生活是件很好的事情，全世界的人们似乎都会赞同这个观点。在美国经济看来陷入衰退、大多数家庭的收入停滞了近10年之时，我们最好能够思考为什么我们需要经济增长。

知识链接

Gallup polls 盖洛普民意测验是美国舆论研究所举办的一种观点的民意测验，它常常被各大媒体用于代表民意的一种表现方式，调查内容包括政治、经济、社会等。这种民意测试的特点是用简单的随机取样法，并且试图把偏差度保持在最低。

题　记

有的人认为钱可以给人安全感；有的人享受购物消费时带来的快乐；有的人喜欢用更多的钱来买更好的奢侈品；有的人觉得有钱就可以进入上层社会，成为受人羡慕和尊敬的人；有的人希望有钱之后可以随心所欲地生活……然而当金钱真的满足这一切时，实际上并没有多少人感到真正的快乐。难道这就是经济学家安德鲁·奥斯瓦德声称的“幸福正在安静地复仇”吗？幸福其实很简单，它不是来自绝对的财富，而是来自相对的财富。幸福是一种感觉，因为幸福的人易于找到配偶，而那些患抑郁症的人以单身居多。幸福是一种爱好、一种兴趣，就好像丘吉尔迷恋油画、爱因斯坦迷恋小提琴，他们在向世人展示，财富与幸福之间的距离依然遥远……

Quiet Revenge

"The happiness," claimed economist Andrew Oswald recently, "are having their quiet revenge." Oswald, a professor at Warwick University in England, is one of a growing number of economists fascinated by the question of what makes us happy. In a recent public lecture he announced, "Once a country has filled its larders①, there is no point in that nation becoming richer." That, at least, should bring a smile to a few faces. Economists have suddenly realized that money can't buy you happiness. This is like the squarest② kid at school suddenly discovering beer, girls and music in his 30s. The rest of the world had worked it out already.

One of the things that excites economists like Oswald is the ability to compare data on wealth, education and marital status with the results of happiness surveys. In these surveys, people are asked such questions as "Taking all things together, would you say you are very happy, quite happy, not very happy, not at all happy?" Economists have been trying

---

① larder [ˈlɑːdə] *n.* 食物橱

② square [skweə] *a.* 正直的

安静的报复

经济学家安德鲁·奥斯瓦德最近声称："幸福正在不动声色地复仇。"奥斯瓦德是英格兰华威大学的教授，当越来越多的经济学家研究是什么使我们幸福时，他就是其中之一。他在最近的一次公开演讲中宣布："一个国家一旦填满了它的食品库，毫无疑问，这个国家就变得更加富裕。"这至少可以给少数面孔带来微笑。经济学家们突然意识到，金钱不能买到幸福。这就像学校里最听话的书呆子，在30岁时才突然发现了啤酒、女孩和音乐。而世界上的其他人早已习以为常。

令奥斯瓦德之类的经济学家们兴奋的问题之一，是能够用幸福调查的结果比较财富、教育和婚姻状况的数据。在这些调查中，他们问这样一些问题："总体来说，你认为你非常幸福、相当幸福、不怎么幸福、还是一点也不幸福？"经济学家们试图通过不同的个人、不同的国家和不同的年代论证有意义的结果。他们列出的头版标题是：一旦一个国家变得相当富裕（即使比美国穷很多），进一步的经济发展似乎并不能增加公民的幸福感。所以，金钱买不到幸福。难道不是这样吗？威尔·威尔金森指出："在任何社会、任何时

to make sense of the results across individuals, across countries and across the years. The headline: Once a country gets fairly rich (though much poorer than the United States), further economic growth does not seem to make its citizens any happier. So, money does not buy happiness. Or does it? "In every society, at any point in time, richer people are happier," points out Will Wilkinson, a policy analyst at the Cato Institute in Washington D.C., who runs a blog on happiness research and public policy. "But that in itself doesn't tell you much about the relationship between money and happiness." Richer people, after all, tend to have high-status jobs. They tend to have more control over their lives at work — why pay someone six figures if you're not going to ask her to use her own judgment? They also have higher expectations and will be comparing themselves to wealthier people. It's hard to say what is really driving the results: money, status or expectations. Perhaps each society's richer people are also happier because happiness comes not from absolute wealth but from relative wealth — recall H.L. Mencken's quip① that "a wealthy man is one who earns $100 a year more than his wife's sister's husband." A more skeptical② view is that while it means something to compare our happiness with that of the guy asking us for change on the street, it means nothing to compare our feelings today to those of our grandfather in 1950 — or those of a Portuguese shopkeeper or a Japanese salary-man.

---

① quip [kwip] *v.* 嘲弄

② skeptical [ˈskeptikəl] *a.* 有争议的

期，更富有的人更幸福。但是它本身并不能说明多少金钱和快乐之间的关系。”威尔金森是位于华盛顿特区卡托研究所的政策分析家，开通了一个幸福研究和公共政策的博客。毕竟，更富有的人倾向于获得地位显赫的工作。他们希望在工作中更多地控制自己的生活：如果你不打算要求某个人采用自己的判断，为什么要为她支付六位数的薪水呢？他们也有更高的希望值，愿意将自己与更富裕的人相比较。很难说到底是什么促成了这种结果：金钱、地位或是期望。或许每一个社会里更富裕的人都比其他人更幸福，因为幸福不是来自绝对的财富，而是来自相对的财富。想想 H.L.孟肯的俏皮话：“一个富有的人是每年能比妻妹的丈夫多挣 100 美元的人。”而争议更大的观点则认为，虽然这意味着把我们的幸福与那些在街上向我们讨钱的人相比较，但若将我们现在的感觉与生活在 20 世纪 50 年代的祖父的感觉相比较，或者与葡萄牙店主或日本上班族相比较，就没有任何意义。

威尔金森、奥斯瓦德之类的经济学家以及他的同胞莱亚德勋爵，正在考虑幸福研究的政策影响。人们的兴趣有些不太一样：新一代研究幸福的经济学家们能给我们提供一些更快乐地生活的建议吗？大多数意见不可靠。例如，已婚的人比单身要幸福得多，所以你就应该结婚吗？如果你的未婚妻妹妹的丈夫失业了，你就会更快乐。不要这么快就下结论。更复杂的调查显示，这两者互为因果：幸福的人易于找到配偶，而那些患抑郁症的人却不太容易找到配偶。毫无疑问，一些人由于婚姻而出类拔萃，而另一些人则痛苦

Wilkinson and economists like Oswald and his compatriot Lord Layard are thinking about the policy implications of happiness research. People's interests vary a little differently: Can the new breed of happiness economists offer us any tips for happier living? Much of the advice is pretty slippery①. For instance, married people are much happier than single people. So perhaps you should get married? Even better if your fiancée's② sister's husband is unemployed. Not so fast. More sophisticated③ surveys show that the causation runs both ways: Happy people tend to find spouses, while those suffering from depression don't find it so easy. And — not surprisingly — some people do brilliantly out of marriage, and others are utterly miserable. There is no idea whether you should propose to that cute girl you've been seeing. You may or may not take comfort in Oswald's finding that you can always get out of marriage: People are happier immediately after a divorce than immediately before.

Oswald also suggests self-employment, if you can pull it off without losing out financially. Everything associated with self-employment — independence, autonomy — is also associated with being happy. Both Oswald and Richard Layard argue that relationships are more important than money — and that includes professional relationships. "I'vecome to believe in the old-fashioned view that one should be tender in one's

---

① slippery [ˈslipəri] *a.* 站不住脚的

② fiancée [ˌfiənˈsei] *n.* 未婚妻

③ sophisticated [səˈfistikeitid] *a.* 复杂的

不堪。你是否应该向你所认识的那位可爱的姑娘求婚还是个未知数。你可能会或不会从奥斯瓦德的发现中得到安慰，这个发现是你随时可以摆脱婚姻：人们在离婚后立即会感觉到比离婚前更幸福。

如果你能做到这一点而经济上又毫发无损，奥斯瓦德还建议你自谋职业。独立、自主权等都与自主创业相关，也与幸福相联系。奥斯瓦德和理查德·莱亚德主张，这种关系比金钱更重要，包括职业关系。莱亚德勋爵在一次交谈中告诉人们："我逐渐相信一种陈旧的观点，一个人和同事在一起时应该对自己的爱人更温柔。从物质上和人际关系以及个人优势两方面想一想你拥有的，而不是你没有的。用经济学的语言来表达，就是不要尝试去纠正不是你的相对优势的事情。"这是一位经济学家在精神层面的思考，但奥斯瓦德用了一个更好的解释。如果你很沮丧，为什么不等待呢？"有一种描述幸福随时间变化的J曲线。30岁晚期是人生中最不快乐的时光，然后越年长越快乐。生命在40岁时再次真正开始。"

最有用的研究来自一位受人尊敬的经济学家：丹尼·卡尼曼，他是唯一获得过诺贝尔经济学奖的心理学家。他询问了近1 000名得克萨斯州的职业妇女，请她们反思以前的日子，列出不同的事件：她们正在做什么，以及她们的感觉如何。有些结果是可以充分预测的：工作很痛苦，而往返上下班更糟糕。其他人的感觉却并不明显。例如，祈祷很有趣，但照看孩子却枯燥乏味。花时间和朋友一起是人们所能做得最享受的事情之一，但花时间和配偶在一起感觉只是还不错。事实上，相比生活中期待的爱人，父母或其他的

dealings with colleagues," Lord Layard told people in an interview. "Think about what you have rather than what you don't have, both materially and in your relationships and your personal strengths. To use the language of economics, don't try to rectify things that aren't your comparative advantage." This is spiritual thinking from an economist, but Oswald goes one better. If you're depressed, why not just wait? "There's a kind of J-curve describing happiness over time. Your late 30s are the most unhappy period of your life, but then the older you get the happier you are. Life really does begin again at 40."

The most useful research, though, is by an honorary economist: Danny Kahneman, the only psychologist ever to win the Nobel Prize in economics. He asked nearly 1,000 working women in Texas to reflect on their previous day, list the different episodes in it, what they were doing and how they were feeling. Some results are predictable enough: Work is miserable, and commuting is worse. Others are not so obvious. For instance, praying is fun, but looking after the kids is not. Spending time with your friends is one of the most enjoyable things you can do, but spending time with your spouse is merely OK. In fact, parents or other relatives turn out to make more enjoyable company than the supposed love of your life. What is perfectly clear, though, is that socializing with anyone except your boss makes you feel good. Sex is best of all. This is handy advice at last. But what if you are having sex with your boss? Whereof economists cannot speak, we must remain silent.

(932 words)

亲戚是更令人愉快的同伴。显而易见的是，与老板以外的任何人打交道都会感觉良好。性爱是最好的，这是最后一条简单适用的建议。但如果你和你的老板发生了性关系会怎样？关于这件事经济学家们不能说，我们必须保持沉默。

知识链接

The Cato Institute 卡托研究所是一个位于美国华盛顿哥伦比亚特区的自由意志主义智库。"卡托"一名来自罗马时代一位捍卫共和国制度的政治家。研究所自许的任务是从"扩展公共政策辩论的角度"参与情报、公共政策以及政府正当角色的讨论。

题 记

难道奉献的精神在我们这个社会已经如此少见、一次慷慨的捐赠竟然成为各大媒体的头条新闻？102 岁的美国老人墨莱思，生前是兼职看门人和干洗店的清洁工，身后却向当地大学捐款 230 万美元。心如黄金的洗衣妇奥莎拉，把一生的积蓄全部奉献给了那些她并不认识、却需要帮助才能完成学业的年轻人。他们之所以被列为创造财富的领袖人物，是因为他们使所有的美国人重新思考和界定他们的奉献能力，是因为他们代表了美国人如何致富的全新思维：我们可以失去财富，但不可以失去智慧；我们可以失去健康，但不可以失去慈悲；我们可以失去家庭，但不可以失去爱心；我们可以失去事业，但不可以失去信仰。我们应该希望自己就是物质财富这个纪念碑上混凝土里的一粒沙子，不要被人记起，但留下的精神财富却让世人共享。

Ordinary People, Extraordinary Wealth

When you think of the wealthy, you may think of yachts and private jets, of mink coats, Jaguars, and mansions① on a hill. Think again, though. As the eye-opening book The Millionaire Next Door revealed, there are many millionaires who walk among us unnoticed. They're common folks like us — with a few quirks②, such as wearing inexpensive suits and staying in the same house for many years. Oh, and having a lot of patience.

Every now and then We run across a story in the news that reminds us of how many fine people there are. It usually happens when one of them dies and surprises the world by giving away a lot of money. It happened just a few months ago, in Montana, when Genesio Morlacci, a 102-year-old former part-time janitor③ and dry cleaner, left $2.3 million to the University of Great Falls. According to an AP story about Mr.

---

① mansion [ˈmænʃən] *n.* 宅第，公馆

② quirk [kwəːk] *n.* 怪癖

③ janitor [ˈdʒænitə] *n.* 看门人

平民百姓的非凡财富

当您想到财富时，您可能会想到游艇和私人飞机、貂皮大衣、捷豹轿车以及山坡上的豪宅。别急，再仔细想想。正如令人瞠目吃惊的《隔壁的百万富翁》一书所揭示的，许多百万富翁就行走在我们中间，并不引人瞩目。他们是和我们一样的普通人，当然他们也有点怪癖，比如，穿着廉价的衣服，多年住在同一所房子里。噢，做事很有耐心。

我们时常在新闻报道中碰到这样的故事，使我们记住了许多好人的行为。他们去世后捐出很多钱，这样的事经常发生，震惊世界。几个月前就发生了这样一件事，蒙大拿州102岁的杰尼西欧·墨莱思向大瀑布大学捐款230万美元，他生前是兼职看门人和干洗店的清洁工。根据美联社的报道，“墨莱思先生是这样一个人，他觉得不需要的东西就不应该购买”。他高度重视教育，因为他从未受过正规教育。“他和妻子露西很少外出吃饭，他们选廉价算餐馆就餐。”他们唯一的奢侈就是去了几趟意大利。我们常常认为，这些故事感人至深，但我们居然没让他们鼓舞我们去采取行动。采取行

Morlacci, "He was a fellow who felt that if you didn't need it, you shouldn't buy it." He valued education highly because he never received a formal education. "On the rare occasions he and his wife, Lucille, dined out, they chose budget restaurants." Their one luxury was a couple of trips to Italy. We often view these stories as inspiring, but we don't let them actually inspire us to take action. Take action! Spend just a few hours per month tending to your financial big picture, and take some steps to ensure a happier retirement① for yourself. While most people depend on the national retirement program to maintain their lives, you can enjoy your twilight years freely.

Another similar story is that of Oseola McCarty, a washerwoman. She once made headlines in newspapers across the country by giving most of her life's savings, $150,000, to the University of Southern Mississippi. Around 1908, Ms. McCarty was born in Mississippi, the pre-Civil-Rights-Movement South. Not only were her means limited but also, quite likely, her dreams. From an early age, Oseola learned the value of a hard-earned dollar. As soon as she could work, she did, ironing clothes, for example. When her aunt fell ill and needed her help, Oseola's formal education was halted after sixth grade. Oseola never married, and she lived for three-quarters of a century in a small, simple house, washing clothes for a living. Not owning a car, she walked everywhere, pushing a shopping cart a mile each way to and from the grocery store. Over the years, she continued to put aside whatever money

① retirement [riˈtaiəmənt] *n.* 退休,退职,退役

动！每个月只花几个小时关注你的金融大版图，采取某些步骤确保自己更幸福地退休吧。大部分人依赖国家的退休计划来维持生活，而你却可以自由自在地享受晚年。

另一个类似的故事是奥莎拉·麦卡迪，一名洗衣妇。她曾登上全国报纸的头条：将一生中的大部分积蓄15万美元捐献给南密西西比大学。麦卡迪女士1908年出生于密西西比州，前南部民权运动的中心。她不仅生活困难，梦想也很可能受到限制。从幼年开始，麦卡迪就知道辛苦得到的钱来之不易。例如，一开始工作，她就熨烫衣服。当她姑姑病倒、需要她照顾时，她不得不在六年级后终止了正规教育。麦卡迪终生未婚，她在一个又小又简陋的房子里生活了四分之三个世纪，以洗衣为生。她没有汽车，推着购物车从杂货店往返一英里到处送衣服。多年来，她坚持把能够攒下的钱零零碎碎地存到当地银行。当银行业务员注意到她的个人储蓄增加到一定程度时，就插手帮她投资，以便她能赚取比储蓄存款账户利息更多的收益。他们把她的钱挪入定期存款和保守的共同基金。他们给她帮了忙吗？当然。他们在非金融方面也对她很照顾。例如，说服她买空调。但是，银行的业务员们能够做得更多吗？也许可以。我们不知道银行业务员们何时注意到她的储蓄，但如果在更早的30年前就已经关注的话，她的捐款最终可能会多很多。她后来似乎攒了约25万美元。而30年前只有5万美元，如果银行业务员帮她投资标普500指数基金，每年赚10.5%，她

she could and plunked[1] her savings into local banks. Her bankers, when they noticed how sizable her savings had grown, stepped in to help her invest it so that she would earn more than savings account interest. They moved her money into the likes of CDs and conservative mutual funds. Did they do her a favor? You bet. They also looked after her in non-financial ways, convincing her to buy an air conditioner, for example. But could the bankers have done more? Perhaps. We don't know when her savings caught their notice, but had it been, say, 30 years earlier, her gift would have ended up a lot bigger. It appears that she had accumulated about a quarter of a million dollars later on. She had only $ 50,000, 30 years earlier. Had the bankers invested her in an S&P 500 index fund, earning, 10. 5% per year, her money would have grown to not $ 250,000 but $ 999,628 — virtually a million dollars. Four times as much.

The lesson here is that in an effort to become your family's most beloved ancestor or a charitable cause's most beloved stranger, you should strive not only to save, but also to invest as foolishly as possible. If Oseola had bought just a few shares of Wal-Mart or General Electric years ago, they would have boosted her bottom line considerably. Indeed, when Ms. McCarty died, one of her bankers wrote to the public, saying: "I have often tried to explain to folks that Miss McCarty's most remarkable feat was living as long as she did. She also found a way to save a little bit of money every week. Time was able to turn even the modest returns of her

---

① plunk [plʌŋk] *vt.* 扑通落下

的钱就不是只增加到 25 万美元，而是999 628美元，近乎 100 万美元，近四倍之多。

这儿的教训是，努力成为家族最受尊敬的长辈或慈善事业最受爱戴的陌生人，你不但要拼命存钱，而且尽可能痴心地投资。如果麦卡迪多年前购买了沃尔玛或通用电气的少许股票，就会大大提高储蓄的底金。事实上，麦卡迪女士去世时，她的一位银行业务员写信告诉公众："我经常试图向人们解释，麦卡迪小姐最非同寻常的壮举就是找到了每星期一点一点省钱的方式。时间能够把她早期微薄的投资转换成几十万美元。如果我们能够在早期建议她购买股票，她将留下数百万的财产而不是只有数十万。"麦卡迪女士后来的捐款令人惊异。捐款时她不希望引人注目。事实上，她是在别人劝说下才放弃匿名的。那接下来发生了什么呢？这位只离开过密西西比州一次的妇女多次前往华盛顿特区和纽约市。她进入白宫，与克林顿会晤，欣喜若狂地参与时代广场新年除夕的水晶球降落仪式。哈佛大学授予她名誉博士学位，萝贝塔·佛莱克为她歌唱，上了"大卫·莱特曼深夜脱口秀"节目，传递奥运火炬。她出现在《纽约时报》的头版，并被芭芭拉·沃尔特斯评为电视台"年度最受欢迎的 10 位公民"之一。

我们承认，所有的这一切都令我们略感震撼。难道奉献的精神在我们这个社会已经如此少见、一次慷慨的捐赠竟然成为全国媒体的头条新闻？虽然我们这些傻瓜知道如何使个人资产收益最大化，

early investments into hundreds of thousands of dollars. If we had been able to introduce her to equities earlier, she would have left millions instead of thousands." The aftermath of Ms. McCarty's gift was amazing. She had not craved attention when she donated her money. In fact, she had to be persuaded to abandon anonymity①. And what happened next? Well, the woman who had left Mississippi only once went to Washington, D.C. and New York City many times. She went to the White House, met the Clintons, and set the Times Square New Year's Eve ball in motion. She received an honorary doctorate from Harvard University, was sung to by Roberta Flack, appeared on "Late Night with David Letterman," and carried the Olympic torch. She was on the front page of The New York Times and was featured on TV as one of "The 10 Most Fascinating People" by Barbara Walters.

We confess that all this makes us shake my head a bit. Has the spirit of giving become so rare in our society that a generous gift makes headlines across the country? While we Fools learn how to best invest our money, we should also give thought to sharing our wealth, both now and later. We should share not only our money, but also our time and our new-found Foolish knowledge. When magnanimity② such as Oseola's becomes a commonplace event, the world will be a better place.

(956 words)

---

① anonymity [ænəˈnimiti] *n.* 匿名

② magnanimity [mægnəˈnimiti] *n.* 宽宏大量

现在和以后也应该考虑分享我们的财富。我们不仅要分享金钱，而且要分享时间和新发现的愚蠢的知识。当奥莎拉之类的慷慨司空见惯之时，世界也会变得更加美好。

知识链接

AP 美国联合通讯社(Associated Press)是美国最大的通讯社，国际性通讯社之一，简称美联社。它由美国报业(1 300家报纸)和广播成员(3 890家电台、电视台)组成，全社工作人员约3 000名，其中编辑、记者1 600多人。国内分社134个(包括6个总分社，100多个分社和记者站)。国外分社83个(包括3个总分社)，驻外记者500人。每天用6种文字播发新闻和经济信息约300万字。

Late Night with David Letterman “大卫深夜脱口秀”是美国哥伦比亚广播公司(CBS)周一到周五晚上十一点至午夜的一档聊天节目。主持人大卫·莱特曼用生动犀利的语言针砭时弊，在嬉笑怒骂中体现地道的娱乐精神，为娱乐类聊天节目树立了榜样。

题 记

经济学意义上的财富定义随着时代的变迁简单而又深刻：具有价值的东西。古希腊的思想家色诺芬、亚里士多德，以及西方经济学的奠基人亚当·斯密，对财富的使用价值都曾做过精辟的论述。然而，在世俗的观念中，人们对纯货币形式的追逐和占有直接影响到人们对财富概念的把握。什么是真正的财富？真正的财富流连于美丽的日落和扑动着翅膀的蝴蝶。我们可以根据游戏的乐趣、邻里之间的社会凝聚力和孩子游戏的品质来衡量财富。我们不可以根据军费开支、战争、监狱的发展、原始森林的砍伐，或增加道琼斯工业平均指数来衡量财富。真正的财富系统是一个工具和过程，它用来衡量或评估所有东西的实际物质和性质条件，使生活有价值。真正的财富评估类似于年度医疗健康检查，提供生活真实财富的总体诊断，实现资产的健康平衡。

A Healthy Balance of Assets

What is wealth? Most of us associate wealth with money, our savings, our investments, our homes or other forms of "financial capital." But did you know that the word wealth comes from the Old English words "weal" (well-being) and "th" (condition) which taken together means "the condition of well-being"? Did you also know that the word "economic" comes from the Greek "oikonomia" meaning "the management of the household." When have you heard a report from economists or business analysts talk about conditions of household living and management? Instead we have become immune to strong language like the word "mortgage" which literally means in French "a pledge unto death" or what I call "a grip of death!" How we have twisted the meaning of words.

Did you know that the father of accounting Lucca Paciolli, a 16th century Franciscan① monk and mathematician, never defined the word "wealth" nor did he provide a definition of "profit." To this day accountants have no clear definition of either word. If real wealth is not just about financial possessions and if accountants have no real

① Franciscan[fræn'siskən] *a.* 圣方济会的

资产的健康平衡

什么是财富？我们大多数人把财富与金钱、积蓄、投资、家庭，或“金融资产”的其他形式联系在一起。但是，你知道 wealth 一词来自古英语单词“weal”（幸福）和“th”（状态），放在一起表示“幸福的状态”吗？你还知道“economic”一词来自于希腊语“oikonomia”，意思是“家庭管理”吗？你什么时候听说过来自经济学家或商业分析师的报告谈论家庭生活和管理状态？相反，我们已经对“mortgage”之类的强硬措词充耳不闻，因为根据法语的字面意思，它表示“死亡誓言”，而我称之为“紧握死亡”！我们是如何扭曲单词含义的呢？

你知道吗，会计之父卢卡·帕索尼是 16 世纪圣方济会的修道士和数学家，他从未给“财富”下定义，也没有给“利润”提供解释。直到今天，会计师们对这两个单词也没有清晰的定义。如果真实的财富不只是金融财产，如果会计师们没有真正理解如何定义、衡量或者解释“真正的”财富，那么，我们拥有一个极好的机会去重新定义和重新发现真实或真正的财富。由于有了重新界定

understanding of how to either define or measure or account for "genuine" wealth then we have a wonderful opportunity to both redefine and rediscover our real or genuine wealth. With that opportunity to redefine "wealth" the "genuine wealth" assessment and management system has been developed. "Genuine" means having the qualities or value claimed authentic. Genuine wealth then are, as Robert Kennedy noted, the things that make life worthwhile. Most of us could define these things in a few minutes.

The genuine wealth system attempts to align① our values and principles as a community with the actual conditions of our wellbeing (personal, professional, spiritual, environmental and financial). Moreover, the genuine wealth system is a tool and process for measuring or assessing the actual physical and qualitative conditions of all the things that make life worthwhile. A genuine wealth assessment is similar to your annual medical checkup, providing a total diagnosis of life's real wealth.

Most of us are accustomed to looking at wealth strictly in financial terms or property and possessions. But real wealth is much more than that, and we know it intuitively. Most of us would define genuine wealth in terms of the conditions of our relationships with our partners, our children, our parents, our friends and our neighbors. We would see genuine wealth in the beauty of a sunset and the flutter② of butterfly wings. We would measure wealth in terms of the joy of our play, the social cohesion of our neighborhoods and the quality of our children's

---

① align [ə'lain] *v.* 使一致

② flutter ['flʌtə] *n.* 鼓翼

“财富”的机会，人们开发了一套“真正财富”的评估和管理系统。“真正”表示主张可信度的品质或价值。那么，正如罗伯特·肯尼迪所指，真正的财富是使生活有价值的东西。我们大多数人在几分钟内就能解释这些东西。

真正财富体系试图将作为整体的价值观和原则与幸福的实际条件（个人、职业、精神、环境和财政）结合起来。此外，真正的财富系统是一个工具和过程，它用来衡量或评估所有东西的实际物质和性质条件，使生活有价值。真正的财富评估类似于年度医疗健康检查，提供生活真实财富的总体诊断。

我们大多数人习惯严格地从金融术语或物业和财产方面看待财富。但是，真正的财富远不止那些，我们在直觉上就明白这一点。我们大多数人根据与合伙人、孩子、父母、朋友和邻居之间的关系状况定义真正的财富。我们可以看到真正的财富流连于美丽的日落和扑动着翅膀的蝴蝶。我们可以根据游戏的乐趣、邻里之间的社交凝聚力和孩子游戏的品质来衡量财富。我们不可以根据军费开支、战争、监狱的发展、原始森林的砍伐，或增加道琼斯工业平均指数来衡量财富。然而，传统的经济学和商业繁荣指标，如GDP（国内生产总值），股票市场指数和其他我们每天都听到的经济指标，与我们将要定义的真正财富无关。事实上，国内生产总值增长等很多指标在经济支出之间没有区别，这种经济实际上对真正的财富发展做出了贡献，与引起“贬值”、或侵蚀社会

play. We wouldn't tend to measure wealth in terms of our military spending, war, the development of prisons, the cutting down of ancient forests, or increases in the Dow Jones Industrial Average. Yet, conventional economics and business indicators of prosperity like GDP (gross domestic product), stock market indices① and other economic indicators that we hear reported daily have little to do with what we would define as genuine wealth. Indeed many of these indicators, like GDP growth, do not distinguish between expenditures in the economy that actually contribute to genuine wealth development versus those which result in the "depreciation" or erosion of our social fabric② or the strength of our relationship with nature. So why do we focus so much on these indicators of "growth" when most of us long for "development" of our relationships with each other and the land?

Another important word is value which comes from the Latin "valorum" which means "to be worthy." Here again we see the confusion of our age. So often we associate value only with monetary expressions (prices, costs, returns on investment) but real value is found in the things that make life worthwhile: genuine wealth. Even a more common word capital has lost its meaning. Capital is actually synonymous with the word wealth defined as "Wealth, in whatever form, used or capable of being used to produce more wealth." If capital means "wealth" and wealth means "the condition of well-being" and capital assets are any form of "wealth" (tangible③ or intangible), then this

---

① indice [ˈindis] *n.* 指数
② fabric [ˈfæbrik] *n.* 结构
③ tangible [ˈtændʒəbl] *a.* 有形的

结构、或我们和自然的关系之力量相冲突。所以，当我们大多数人渴望“发展”与他人和土地之间的关系时，为什么要如此关注这些“增长”指数呢?

另一个重要单词是价值，它来自拉丁语“valorum”，意思是“值得”。在此，我们再次看到了时代的混乱。因此，我们经常只将价值与货币表现（价格、成本、投资回报）相连，但是，真正的价值建立在使生活有价值的东西之上，即真正的财富。即使更常见的单词资本也已经失去了它的本义。资本实际上是单词财富的同义词，定义为“财富，无论以何种形式，用以或能够被用来产生更多的财富”。如果资本的意思是“财富”，财富的意思是“幸福的条件”，而资本资产是“财富”的任意形式（有形的或无形的），那么，这意味着一个新的方法，同时衡量和管理实际财富或实际资本。

实际资本或“生活资本”是资产或每个人的各个方面，即所谓的“人力”资本，与社会资本和自然资本如影随形。人力资本一般定义为“知识、技能、能力和其他的个体属性，推动个人、社会和经济福利的创造”。在北美本土文化中，人类归属于四个方面：情绪、身体、精神和心理。一个完整的人具备这些核心资产或能力的健康平衡。我们通过“意志”（我们的意志力）使用这些资产，追逐我们的愿景和对美好生活的梦想。社会资本是人与人之间关系的价值。根据定义，社会资本表示“推动集体行为的关系、网络和规

suggests a new approach to both the measurement and management of real wealth or real capital.

Real capital or "life capital" are the assets or aspects of each human being — so-called "human" capital — along with social and natural capital. Human capital is generally defined as "the knowledge, skills, competencies, and other attributes of each individual that facilitates the creation of personal, social, and economic well-being." In the indigenous① cultures of North America, there are four aspects of a human being: emotional, physical, spiritual and mental. A complete human being has a healthy balance of these core assets or capabilities. We exercise these assets through "volition" (our will power) in pursuing our vision or dream of the good life. Social capital is the value of relationships we have with each other. By definition social capital means the "relationships, networks and norms that facilitate collection action" that include such things as social cohesion and forma and informal institutional arrangements. Natural capital is the natural resource or environmental assets and systems that provide humanity with nature's materials and services that are vital to economic wellbeing.

(877 words)

---

① indigenous [in'didʒinəs] *a.* 土著的,本土的

范”，包括社会凝聚力、形式和非正式的体制安排。自然资本指自然资源、或环境资产和制度，给人类提供自然原料和服务，这些都是至关重要的经济福祉。

知识链接

The Dow Jones Industrial Average 道琼斯工业指数是世界上最有影响、使用最广的一种算术平均股价指数，已成为世界金融文化的代号。它的计算公式为：股票价格平均数=入选股票的价格之和/入选股票的数量。该指数目的在于反映美国股票市场的总体走势，涵盖金融、科技、娱乐、零售等多个行业。

题 记

是什么使我们快乐？新兴领域“积极心理学”中的许多新发现表明，人们的一举一动能对快乐感以及满足感产生显著的影响。哲学家们一直以来试图说服人们相信：真正的幸福在于对内心深处既定目标的追求，而不是对短暂的快乐和财产的追求。人类具有放弃直接的满足感、追求某种更深层次的满足感的能力，但获得这方面的幸福需要意志力。那些能为某些有意义的事情——不论是学习一门新手艺或者提高孩子的道德意识，而献身努力的人们比起那些没什么强烈的梦想和抱负的人要快乐得多。无论是在迪拜的黄金市场，或是在人烟稀少的澳大利亚，幸福早已超越了基因和环境，满足的程度不会随着需求的实现显著提高。作为人类，我们非常需要存在的意义。

A Barometer of Sadness

Americans have seen their retirement savings shrivel, home equity evaporate and job security vanish. The only numbers zooming upward seem to be gas and food prices. It may look like there's nothing to smile about, but that shouldn't stop us, said Ed Diener, a psychology professor at the University of Illinois at Urbana-Champaign who has been studying happiness for more than a quarter-century. Here's what he wants you to know: That disappearing 401 (k) balance? It's no more a barometer① of sadness than winning the lottery guarantees life satisfaction. It's all a matter of perspective. There are people who have little money and are quite happy, and then there are people who feel poor making $ 150,000 a year. Diener said: "If we ratchet down some of our aspirations and expectations, we can find contentment — even in a slowing economy." He is no blithe guru spray-painting smiley faces along Wall Street. Researchers like Diener are trying to convey what philosophers have long written: True happiness lies in the pursuit of deeply held goals, not in fleeting② pleasures and possessions.

Diener is co-author, with his son, Robert Biswas-Diener, of the

---

① barometer [bəˈrɔmitə] *n.* 晴雨表

② fleeting [ˈfliːtiŋ] *adj.* 飞逝的，短暂的

伤心的晴雨表

美国人眼睁睁地看着他们的退休储蓄在缩减，家庭资产在蒸发，就业保障在消失。唯一急剧上涨的似乎就是天然气和食品价格。伊利诺伊大学厄本那-香槟分校的一位心理学教授爱德华·迪纳认为，看起来这并不值得高兴，但也不应该对我们形成障碍。25年多来，他一直致力于研究幸福。以下是他希望你知道的：401（k）养老金的平衡消失了吗？与其说它是伤心的晴雨表，还不如说它是赢彩票来保证对生活的满意度。它完全是一件深谋远虑的事。很多人没什么钱但是很快乐，而有些人每年赚15万美元还在叫穷。迪纳说："如果我们降低一些愿望和期待，即使是在经济增长缓慢的情况下，也会找到满足感。"他并非是华尔街上佯装笑脸、漠不关心的专家。迪纳这样的研究人员正在力图传达哲学家们一直以来的说教：真正的幸福在于对内心深处既定目标的追求，而不是对短暂的快乐和财产的追求。

迪纳和儿子罗伯特·比斯瓦斯·迪纳合著了一本新书："幸福：解开心理财富的秘密"。迪纳认为，将拥有心理财富的人与可怜的同龄人区分开的是他们的协调能力。他声称："这就是说，控制能够控制的，将你的股票多样化，然后回归一帆风顺的生活，如朋友

new book "Happiness: Unlocking the Mysteries of Psychological Wealth." What separates those with psychological wealth from miserable peers is their ability to adjust, Diener believes. "That means controlling what is controllable, diversifying your stocks, then returning to the areas of your life that are going well, such as friends and family," he said. "It means making a conscious decision to be resilient."

It takes strong character to find happiness in the face of adversity, but scientists often have found that aspect too vague a topic to study. Understanding how the brain processes raw feelings of desire and pleasure is far easier. Most creatures seek pleasure in some way. Pleasure motivates us to seek food, sex and a multitude of things that ensure the survival of an individual or species. "There's an enormous evolutionary advantage to getting pleasure from these things," said Martin Cassell, a professor at the University of Iowa. "The more long-term aspects of what causes happiness are much less well understood." Cassell believes a key brain area for both pleasure and long-term happiness is the insular cortex, a region buried under the flaps and folds toward the front of the brain. Also called the insula①, the region has been linked to sensations of joy, disgust and pain and even to out-of-body experiences.

But beyond joy, a hallmark of human beings is the ability to forgo immediate gratification for the sake of some deeper contentment. That aspect of happiness takes willpower — another big subject neuroscientists have found difficult to study. "We have no precise sense of what willpower means in the brain, or why some people are better at it than others," said Todd Braver, a professor of psychology and neuroscience

---

① insula [ˈinsjulə] *n.* 脑岛

和家庭。这就意味着要有意识地做决定，使生活富有弹性。”。

面对逆境寻找幸福需要坚强的性格，但科学家们通常发现，这个方面太模糊了，难以作为专题对其进行研究。而了解大脑如何处理欲望和快乐的原始感觉就要容易得多。大多数动物以某种方式寻找快乐。快乐促使我们去寻找食物、性和大量确保我们作为个体或物种生存下去的东西。爱荷华大学的马丁·卡塞尔教授说:“我们有巨大的进化优势从这些东西中获得快乐。越能带来长远幸福的事物越难以被理解。”卡塞尔认为，快乐和长期幸福的关键大脑区域是孤立的皮层，一块朝向大脑的前方、埋在皮瓣和褶皱中的区域。它也被叫做脑岛，这块区域与快乐、厌恶和痛苦的感觉、甚至与体外的感受联系在一起。

但是在快乐之外，人类的一个特征就是具有放弃直接的满足感、追求某种更深层次的满足感的能力。获得这方面的幸福需要意志力，这是另一个神经科学家发现很难研究的课题。圣路易斯华盛顿大学的心理学教授和神经学科学家托德·布瑞维指出:“我们对于意志力在大脑里的表现缺乏精确的判断力，即为什么有些人的意志力比其他人更强大。”布瑞维的团队正在研究称之为前额皮层的大脑区域是如何参与长期决策的。他们想了解对遥远未来奖赏的预期如何拒绝短期快乐的诱惑，诸如充满成就感、但报酬很低的工作增加的满意度。

人类行为和幸福的奥秘一直是迪纳家庭晚餐交谈的主要话题。62 岁的迪纳也被称为“快乐博士”，在香槟分校的早期婚姻期间，他有大量的机会思考幸福的本质，当时他和同是心理学家的妻子罗尔一起外出吃饭只点 1 美元的主菜。他们的五个孩子有三个进入了

at Washington University in St. Louis. Braver's team is studying how the brain area called the prefrontal cortex is involved in long-term decision-making. They want to understand how the anticipation of a reward far off in the future — such as the increased satisfaction of a fulfilling but low-paying job — can sometimes overrule① the enticement of short-term pleasure.

The mysteries of human behavior and happiness have long dominated Diener family dinner conversations. Diener, 62, also known as "Dr. Happy," had ample opportunity to reflect on the nature of happiness during his early marriage years in Champaign, when dining out meant a $1 entree② with his wife, Carol, also a psychologist. Three of their five children went into the family business, including Robert, a psychologist and lecturer at Portland State University. The father and son have traveled all over the world, collecting data on well-being from tens of thousands of subjects in more than 100 countries.

Whether in the gold markets of Dubai or the Australian outback, the scientists have learned happiness goes beyond genes and circumstances. We require enough material wealth to be self-sufficient, the psychologists believe, but the levels of contentment do not dramatically increase after our needs are met. While there is a spike after a major acquisition — like a new car — the euphoria③ over leather seats doesn't last.

(696 words)

---

① overrule [əuvəˈruːl] *vt.* 推翻,驳回

② entree [ˈɑntre] *n.* 主菜

③ euphoria[juːˈfɔːriə] *n.* 精神欢快,兴高采烈

家族事业，其中包括波特兰州立大学的心理学家和讲师罗伯特。父亲和儿子已经环游了世界，在100多个国家、从数以万计的受试者中收集有关幸福的数据。

无论是在迪拜的黄金市场，或是在人烟稀少的澳大利亚，科学家们已经认识到，幸福超越了基因和环境。我们需要足够的物质财富自给自足，但是心理学家们认为，满足的程度不会随着需求的实现显著提高。尽管满足感在一次大规模的获取后仍会飙升，如一部新车，但对皮座椅表现出的极度兴奋并不会持续很久。

知识链接

401(k) 401(k)计划作为“雇员福利”项目之一的养老金计划一直是美国人生活中不可或缺的组成部分，它允许员工将一部分税前工资存入一个储蓄计划，积累至退休后使用。

题　记

吝啬鬼永远是世界文学作品中亦喜亦悲的角色。英国莎士比亚喜剧《威尼斯商人》中的夏洛克，法国莫里哀喜剧《悭吝人》中的阿巴贡，法国巴尔扎克小说《欧也妮·葛朗台》中的葛朗台，以及俄国文学大师果戈理小说《死魂灵》中的泼留希金。面对金钱，吝啬鬼得到的仅仅是满足感，他并没享受到拥有金钱的快乐。吝啬鬼给人类留下了两个教训：一个教训是，金钱是达到目的的手段；另一个教训是，净资产如果保护不当就可能丢失。真正能够体验金钱快乐的人，是那些善于运用金钱来享受和增加财富的人。利用财富达到自己的目标和实现自己理想，才是财富真正的价值所在，也是幸福的源泉！所以，要想从金子中获得快乐，就必须设立自己的目标，让财富实现它真正的价值。

How Could the Miser Have Been Better Off

What do you think about when you hear the word wealth? I bet most of you conjured[①] up images like Donald Trump, a mansion from MTV Cribs, or Scrooge McDuck swimming in his money bin. And that's perfectly in line with what most people think. When I do a Google image search for wealth, some of the first results are money, a mansion with a pool, a fancy sports car, and my favorite, a rich family in a country club toasting champagne over a flower centerpiece.

What this tells me is that we generally think of wealth as the ability to do expensive activities. In other words, wealth means having a high net worth. Net worth is an important wealth measure to government agencies and academic researchers. Net worth is often the primary wealth measure because it is easy to calculate, it increases when people do good things like save more or earn more, and it is a key determinant of status. There are many resources to improve your net worth like NetworthIQ, a community of bloggers who dispense tips about your career,

---

① conjure [ˈkʌndʒə] *vi.* 想象,联想起

吝啬鬼怎样才能过得更好

听到财富一词，你会想什么？我敢打赌，大多数人肯定会突发奇思妙想，大脑里出现音乐电视《婴儿床》中的摩天大楼唐纳德·特朗普的形象，或者像史高治·麦克老鸭那样，在他那装满了钞票的钱柜里游泳的人。这完全符合大多数人的所思所想。我在谷歌图片库中搜索财富一词时，一些排在首页的搜索结果是金钱、附带游泳池的大厦、豪华的跑车以及我特别喜欢的画面：一个富豪家庭在乡村俱乐部里围坐在中央放置花篮的餐桌旁高举香槟祝酒。

从中我可以得知，我们通常想到的财富就是举办昂贵活动的能力。换句话说，财富代表拥有高净值。净资产是政府机构和学术研究人员量度财富的重要工具。因为净资产容易计算，它常常是首要的财富标准，钱存得越多或挣得越多，人就会处于良性循环的状态，净资产就会增加，净资产是社会地位的决定因素。有很多资源增加你的净资产，如 NetworthIQ 博客社区，它能给你提供职业、投资和储蓄策略方面的建议。

令人感到宽慰的是，拥有中等资本净值的美国人的数量在过去 20 年间呈稳定增长之势。那么，我们感到更快乐吗？研究结果各

investments, and saving strategies.

And there is a comforting trend: The median net worth in America has been steadily increasing over the past twenty years. So are we happier? Studies are mixed, but overall, it doesn't appear so. Americans are less happy now than thirty years ago due to longer work hours. Even more disconcerting① is that joint study in the periodical Science shows that richer people now are not much happier "moment-to-moment" than less wealthy individuals. The authors even say "effect of income on life satisfaction seems to be transient." What is going on? Why doesn't higher net worth translate to more happiness? I think part of the answer has been known since at least Ancient Greek in the writings of Aesop in the story of The Miser and his Gold: Once upon a time there was a Miser who used to hide his gold at the foot of a tree in his garden; but every week he used to go and dig it up and gloat over his gains. A robber, who had noticed this, went and dug up the gold and decamped with it. When the Miser next came to gloat over his treasures, he found nothing but the empty hole. He tore his hair, and raised such an outcry that all the neighbors came around him, and he told them how he used to come and visit his gold. "Did you ever take any of it out?" asked one of them. "Nay," said he, "I only came to look at it." "Then come again and look at the hole," said a neighbor; "it will do you just as much good." Wealth unused might as well not exist.

I take away two main lessons from the story about why the Miser's

① disconcerting [ˌdiskənˈsəːtiŋ] *adj.* 令人不安的,令人惊惶的

不相同，但总体上并非如此。由于工作时数更长，美国人现在比30年前的快乐指数更低。令人感到困惑的是，《科学》杂志的联合研究显示，更富裕的人现在并非“每时每刻”比那些不那么富裕的人更快乐。研究者们甚至说：“收入给生活带来的满足感似乎很短暂。”到底发生什么事了？为什么更高的资本净值不能转化成更幸福的感觉？我认为，部分答案至少在古希腊哲人伊索的作品《吝啬鬼与他的金子》中就已经揭晓：从前有一个吝啬鬼，总是把他的金子藏在花园的树下。每个星期他都会去把它挖出来，心满意足地看着他的财富。一个抢劫犯看到了，就去把金子挖出来逃走了。当吝啬鬼再次得意扬扬地来看他的财宝时，什么都没有了，只剩下一个空落落的大洞。他扯着自己的头发，声嘶力竭地大声喊叫着，所有的邻居都出来了，围在他的周围，他告诉邻居们，他过去是如何过来看他的金子的。其中的一个邻居问道：“你拿出来过一块金子吗？”他说：“没有。我只是过来看看它而已。”一个邻居说：“那就再来看一下那个洞好了，跟你过去来看金子一样啊。”财富如果被弃之不用就相当于从未存在过。

我从这个故事中得到两个主要的教训，明白了为什么吝啬鬼的金子（他的高净值）没能给他带来快乐：一个教训是，金钱是达到目的的手段。资本净值告诉你，你有多少钱，但并不是要你享用这些钱。另一个教训是，净资产如果保护不当（风险投资或保险缺损）就可能丢失。吝啬鬼的愚蠢之处就是把钱藏在树下，很容易被强盗偷走。有些人现在只是很愚蠢地保护着自己的资产，让自己遭受阴险的首席执行官之类的现代抢劫犯的掠夺。

gold (his high net worth) did not lead to happiness. One is that money is a means to an end. Net worth informs you on how much money you have, not whether you are enjoying the money. Another one is that net worth can be lost if poorly protected (risky investments or lack of insurance). The Miser was foolish to put his money in the tree since it was easily stolen by the robber. Some people today are just as foolish protecting their assets, leaving them prey to modern robbers like shady CEOs.

How could the Miser have been better off, and what can you do about it? For starters, redefine wealth as financial fulfillment, and then start writing specific goals. Goals help you answer: why do you want money? It is usually to accomplish something you want now, like to buy an engagement ring, or get an Apple iPhone, or to pay off credit card debt. But you likely also want money for the future to buy a beach side house in Hawaii and support your children's education.

For me, wealth is simply accomplishing these financial goals. Naturally, before I can accomplish them, I spend a few minutes to write them down. This is perhaps the most important step you can take in acquiring wealth. I write down short-term goals for the next three to six months, followed by medium term goals of one to five years, followed by long term goals. I try to make the goals precise so I have a plan of action, and of course, I review the goals a couple times a year. I started writing goals during high school and still have the records with me. To give you flavor, here are a couple short to medium term goals I wrote down during college: — By graduation, be knowledgeable in investments other than stocks. — Look into jobs. Start considering what I want to do and how I

吝啬鬼怎样才能过得更好，你能采取什么办法？ 对刚入门的人来说，要把财富重新定义为财富满足感，之后开始考虑写下详细的目标。目标帮助你回答：你为何需要金钱？ 金钱常常帮你完成现在想做的事，如买个订婚戒指，买个苹果的iPhone，或付清信用卡债务。又或者你可能需要钱在将来买一幢夏威夷的海滨别墅，或者是提供孩子受教育的费用。

对我来说，财富只不过是要完成这些财务目标。在做到这些之前，我花几分钟的时间就自然而然地把它们写了下来。这可能是你取得财富要采取的最重要的步骤。我写下了下一个3至6个月的短期目标，之后1至5年的中期目标，还有长期目标。我试图把目标精细化，这样我才能有一个行动计划，当然，我会在一年中进行几次目标评估。我在高中的时候开始记录这些目标，仍然保存着这些记载。为了给你帮助，我把大学时写的短期到中期的目标给你看看：毕业时，除股票外，要深入了解投资方面的知识。找工作。开始思考我要做什么，我怎么能找到令我满意的高薪工作。

很欣慰，我已经完成了这些目标。把目标写下来并制订计划把我推到了正确的道路上。我通过读书、上课以及向更富有的亲属求教他们如何理财，变得更加博学，从而完成了第一个目标。只是通过不断地提问就能学到这么多知识，真是令人感到惊讶。我并没有提那些最尖锐的问题，但人们都非常友好，因为他们被我这个年龄的人提出的问题所感染。我利用大学就业中心，参加了各种各样的招聘会，和那些对自己工作很满意的人交谈，实现了第二个目标。由于指导老师坦诚的建议，我根据自己的学术水准，最后决定到一

can find a high paying job that satisfies it.

I am happy to say I've accomplished these goals. The act of writing them and having a plan pushed me in the right path. In the first goal, I became more knowledgeable through reading books, taking classes, and asking my richer relatives how they manage their money. It is amazing how much you can learn simply by asking. I didn't have the sharpest questions, but people were very helpful since they were impressed some one my age was asking. For the second goal, I used my college's career center, went to various job fairs, and talked to people I knew who were enjoying their jobs. I eventually decided on a corporate job over academia① thanks to candid② advice from my advisor. And I got a really great job since I focused on what I wanted to do instead of how much money the job would offer. I eliminated certain high-paying jobs and focused on the jobs I would actually enjoy. Did eliminating jobs like investment banking lower my net worth? Absolutely. And I don't care. Since I enjoyed my job that paid reasonably well, I was able to get some thing better: achieve wealth.

(1,000 words)

---

① academia [ˌækəˈdimiə] *n.* 学术界,学术环境
② candid [ˈkændid] *adj.* 公正的,坦白的,率直的

家公司工作。 因为我关注我想干什么而不是工作可以提供多少钱，我得到了一份真正了不起的工作。 我拒绝了某些高薪工作，集中做我真正喜欢的工作。 拒绝高薪工作就像投资银行降低了我的资本净值吗？ 绝对是的，但我不在意。 因为我很享受我的工作，收入也还不错，我可以把一些事做得更好：积聚财富。

知识链接

Scrooge McDuck 史高治·麦克老鸭有橙黄色的嘴、脚和蹼，是迪士尼所创的经典动画角色之一。史高治被塑造成全世界最富有的老鸭，然而他仍不断去扩充自己的财富。“史高治”的含义是吝啬鬼、守财奴和贪得无厌之徒。“守财奴”史高治·麦克老鸭在《福布斯》15 位最富有虚拟人物榜中高居榜首，它囤积了估价达 441 亿美元的金币。

题　记

毋庸讳言，我们处于一个西方精神贫乏与东方物质贫困的时代。西方世界里的精神贫乏以国会大厦哗众取宠的声音、电视广播毒药般的花言巧语、商人政客虚伪的假笑冲撞着人们的良心与意志。东方世界里的物质贫困则以一种朴素而客观的方式存在着，贫困家庭的生活水平达不到一种社会可以接受的最低标准，贫困人口缺少获取和享有正常生活的能力。然而，也从来没有任何时代像今天这样给那些真正具有良知、使命感、道德感和拯救意识的年轻人带来如此巨大的挑战和契机。当一群年轻的学生以传教士的身份投入到修女们的慈善工作中时，他们的灵魂受到了洗礼，他们的世界观得到了升华。特雷莎修女的箴言深深嵌入了他们的脑海：如果你找到了平静和幸福，他们可能会嫉妒你。不管怎样，你还是要快乐；你今天做的善事，人们往往明天就会忘记。不管怎样，你还是要做善事。

Spiritual Poverty of the West vs. Material Poverty of the East

There was a little nun in Tijuana who had very wise eyes. Their glance was sharp and critical, and the eyebrows over them arched frequently; but the light in them was unmistakable. It was the light of eyes used to gazing in love. She adeptly① avoided giving us her name, and as curious as we were about her, we never asked. Anyway, they were all "Sister" to us. This little nun in particular was on retreat for most of our stay there, and so we didn't meet her until the very last working night of our trip, and then, only a few of us.

My fellow student missionaries② Sarah, Mary, Mandy, and I were elected to go with the Sisters out to the coast, along the very cliffs of which Tijauna washes up a second sea of tiny shanties, each stacked against the other haphazardly. Most of the work the Sisters had us help them with was easy work, except for the toil of washing barrels and

---

① adept [əˈdept] *a.* 熟练的，内行的

② missionary [ˈmiʃənəri] *n.* 传教士

西方的精神贫乏与东方的物质贫困

提华纳有一个小修女，她的双眼闪烁着明亮的智慧。炯炯的目光尖锐而挑剔，眼上的眉毛常常挑起成半月形，但眼中的目光却清纯无瑕。这种目光充满爱意的凝视。她轻巧地绕开提及她的名字，虽然我们对她分外好奇，但也从来不问。不管怎样，她们对我们来说就是“修女”。我们大多数人在的时候，小修女都会故意离开，所以直到此行的最后一个晚上，我们也没怎么碰见她。就连之后，也只有很少人见过她。

我的同行者——都是学生身份的传教士莎拉、玛丽、曼蒂被挑选出来，和一些修女前往海岸。提华纳掀起的海浪又一次扑向沿着岸边悬崖修建的简陋棚屋，它们相互支撑，东倒西歪。修女们让我们帮忙做的大多数事情很简单，但也有用手一桶又一桶地洗衣这种脏活累活，这样的琐事让我们花费了整个早上的时间帮助我们驻地的那些无家可归的老年妇女，修女们称呼她们为“老奶奶”。但这种工作从另一个角度讲也很困难，因为它需要我们这些年轻、金发

barrels of laundry by hand, a chore that made up our mornings in the house for homeless elderly women — "the Grandmas", as the Sisters called them — where we stayed. But this kind of work was difficult in another way, because it entailed we young, blonde, wealthy American girls looking into the faces of women who couldn't always promise their children supper; and seeing only gratitude, and feeling immensely humbled.

This little nun seemed to make up her mind, as soon as she got in the van with us that she was going to give us something we could take home with us. She did this by sharing her mind with us, by talking incessantly. She spoke her every observation out loud, she told us about her childhood in India, about her family and her discovery of her vocation, about the most nuanced① differences of culture — differences she said were impossible to explain to her mother in letters, but which she made wonderfully clear to us, although English was her ninth language.

When I was sitting on the floor of the van with her I felt obliged to respond, but for a time the other girls fell absolutely quiet, reflecting on her words. After a while I also gave up asking questions, because there was an enormous lump in my throat, although I don't remember exactly what it was she was discoursing on when I became so overwhelmed. The totality of the picture she painted for us, together with the extraordinary

① nuanced [njuːˈɑːnst] *a.* 有细微差别的

碧眼、富裕的美国女孩面对那些连孩子的晚餐都无法保障的母亲，我们看到的全是感激之情，真的感到非常惭愧。

这个小修女似乎下定决心，她一坐上我们的大篷车，就打算送一些东西让我们带回家。她用这种方式与我们交流思想，不停地讲话。她把她观察到的每一个细节都大声讲出来，她告诉我们她在印度度过的童年，她的家人和她怎样发现了自己的使命。她说，最细微的文化差异甚至在给母亲的信中都无法解释，虽然英语是她的第九语言，但她却能够使我们非常清楚她的表白。

当我和她一起坐在大篷车的地板上时，我不得不做出一些回应。有一会儿，其他女孩都鸦雀无声，思考着她谈话的内容。过了一会，我也没有再问，因为我的喉咙就像被一个巨大的肿块堵住了一般，虽然我无法准确地记住当时她说了些什么使我变得如此不堪重负。她为我们描绘的所有画面、还有眼中非同寻常的光芒，这一切都是那样的美丽，我无法用言语在这儿表达出来，她的目光偶尔停留在我们中的一个身上，然后平静地望向窗外。然而，我还是想请教她一个问题，她的回答也值得分享。我问道："小妹妹，你在东方印度看到的贫困和你在这里看到的有没有大的差异？"

她睁大眼睛看着我，然后点了点头。"哦"，她深呼吸了一下，"这不是一回事"。她说，在印度，物质贫困远远比她在西方的任何地方看到的都要严重得多，所以她在这里看到的从来没有什么给她留下非常深刻的印象。这里的人们遭受贫困，但他们不会为此而

light in that gaze that she occasionally fixed on one of us, before shifting her gaze calmly out the window, was too beautiful for my own words to represent here. There was one question, however, that I thought to ask her, which gained a response worth sharing. "Sister," I asked, "is there a great difference between, say, the kind of poverty you saw in the East, in India, and what you see here?"

Her eyes widened at me, and she nodded. "Ohhhh," she breathed. "It is not the same thing at all." She said that in India, material poverty is much, much greater than anything she's seen in the West, and so she is never really impressed by what she sees here. Here, people suffer from poverty, but they do not die just from it; there they will die tomorrow if they do not get food.

But, she said, in the East, the soul is different. It is stronger, as she put it, and solid. Whether a person is Christian, or Hindu, or Muslim, or Buddhist, he is a solid Christian, a solid Hindu, Muslim, or Buddhist. He will not lose faith because he is hungry, or because he is well-fed. And in India, if people are hungry, they are still happy. The poorest people on the streets, she said, are the happiest. If they have food today, they are happy; they do not wonder if they will have food tomorrow. Their joy, she insisted, is something unlike anything you see on any face in the West.

In the West, it is different. Here most poor people have enough, even though they don't understand how little "enough" is. But they are unhappy, she said and she knelt to look through the rear window at the

死，但在东方，人们如果得不到食物，第二天就会死掉。

但是她说，东方人的灵魂是不同的，就像她说的那样，更加坚强、更加牢固。一个人，不管他是基督徒，或印度教徒，或穆斯林信徒，或佛教信徒，他都是坚定的基督徒、印度教徒、穆斯林信徒、佛教信徒。他不会因为饥饿或营养充足而失去信仰。在印度，人们就算忍饥挨饿也仍然快乐。她说，街上最穷的人也是最快乐的人。如果他们今天有吃的，他们会开心；他们不会去想明天是否有吃的。她坚持认为，他们的喜悦完全不同于你在西方人脸上看到的喜悦。

西方就不同了。这儿的大多数穷人有足够的食物，即使他们不理解“足够”是多少。但是他们不幸福，她边说边跪下来，透过后窗凝视围在大篷车后的那些母亲们疲惫的脸，其他的修女们在分发食物前正引导他们在圣母玛丽亚的像前做祈祷。他们不快乐，因为他们没有信仰。这是真正的贫穷。她补充说，在美国你越往北走，会觉得越来越富有，但快乐却越来越少。她严肃地看着我们说，这些人沮丧而悲哀，“没有信仰只有一幢豪华的大房子”，他们是穷人中最贫穷的人。这就是特雷莎修女的意思。

我们在提华纳的一周内，与小修女在一起的时间仅仅只有三小时，但在这期间，我们看到了和感受到了以前从未遇到过的事情，这种经历似乎重塑了我们的人生。修女似乎明白了我们在这个星期之后的心情，也知道我们从哪里来，要回到哪里去。她理解我们。

tired faces of the mothers gathered outside the van, as the other Sister led them in Santa Marias before distributing their food. They are unhappy, because they have no God. That is the real poverty. The farther North you go in America, she added, the more wealth you see, and the less joy you find. Those people, she said, looking seriously at us, the depressed, and the sad people "with no God and a great big house", are the poorest of the poor. That's what Mother Teresa meant.

Our experience of this little nun lasted but three hours of our week in Tijuana, during which we saw and felt many things we'd never seen or felt before, and tried to let ourselves be molded by our experiences. Sister seemed to understand our frame of mind at the end of such a week, and where we came from, and what we were going back to. She understood us. She wanted to impart① to us an understanding of why we had come to Tijuana. As far as Sister was concerned, we had come so that our imaginations could be imprinted with some visible image — like the feeding, and the clothing, and the visiting of the poor — of the missionary work we are supposed to be doing spiritually, all the time, to all those around us.

(939 words)

---

① impart [ɪmˈpɑːt] *vt.* 给予,传授,告知

她希望传递给我们一种想法，我们为什么要来提华纳。 就修女而言，我们来了，某些明显的意象就可能在脑海中留下烙印，如吃饭、穿衣和拜访穷人，我们应该从精神上做一些传教士的工作，随时随地帮助我们周围需要帮助的人。

知识链接

Tijuana 提华纳是墨西哥西北边境的一座旅游城市，位于美国加利福尼亚州的西北端，北距圣地亚哥市 19 公里。

Mother Teresa 特雷莎修女(Mother Teresa of Calcutta，1910 年 8 月 27 日—1997 年 9 月 5 日)是世界著名的天主教慈善工作者，主要替印度加尔各答的穷人服务。因其一生奉献给解除贫困，而于 1979 年获得诺贝尔和平奖。她也是诺贝尔奖百余年历史上最受尊崇的 3 位获奖者之一(其他两位是 1921 年物理学奖得主阿尔伯特・爱因斯坦、1964 年和平奖得主马丁・路德金)。

题　记

GDP的增长与人民生活水平不同步的变化让人们对这一衡量国民经济发展情况的重要指标深感怀疑。GDP统计本身存在一定的缺陷，主要表现在：一是正面因素，即社会进步，科技发展，生产要素投入的增加促进了生产的发展，使GDP增长；二是为消除负面影响而进行的生产活动，也可以促进GDP增长。例如，不清洁生产造成环境污染，水土流失，而治理环境污染的生产活动又形成新的GDP。GDP没有将正面的建设性和负面的破坏性活动区别开来，也没有明确考虑主要由污染而导致的环境质量下降，以及随之而来的对人类健康和财富的影响。因此，只一味追求GDP的增长，并不能从根本上提高人民的生活水平。

An Imperfect Link

Does money buy happiness? This week, Senator Byron Dorgan, Democrat of North Dakota, will join a long line of people who have taken serious stabs at trying to answer that thorny question. He will hold a hearing exploring whether traditional economic measures like per-capita income accurately capture people's sense of well-being.

This has long been a contested issue. Although everyone concedes① that income is an imperfect welfare measure, conservative economists have tended to emphasize its virtues while liberals have been more likely to stress its shortcomings. The debate is not just of philosophical interest; it also has important policy implications. Recent research findings offer support for specific arguments on both sides. Mounting evidence suggests, however, that per-capita income is a less reliable measure of well-being when income inequality has been rising rapidly, as it has in recent decades. First, a few words about how economists measure income: The most commonly used metric is gross domestic product, the

① concede [kənˈsiːd] v.(勉强)承认

玷污的纽带

钱能买来幸福吗？ 这个星期，北达科他州的民主党参议员拜伦·多根，将加入在回答那个棘手的问题上遭遇挫折的一长队人中。 他将就传统的经济学指标，如人均收入是否准确地反映了人们的幸福感召开听证会。

这一直是个有争议的问题。尽管每个人都承认收入是一个有缺陷的社会福利指标，保守的经济学家们强调它的优点，而自由主义者则紧盯其缺点。 这场辩论不仅具有哲学上的意义，还具有重要的决策启示。 目前的研究结果支持双方的具体论据。 越来越多的证据表明，不管怎样，当收入差距不断拉大时，像在近几十年中，人均收入不是衡量福利的一个可靠的标准。 首先我们来看看经济学家是如何估量收入的：最常用的标尺是国内生产总值，即一个国家或地区的经济中所生产出的全部最终产品和劳务的价值。 人均 GDP 就是 GDP 除以总人口数，以2 000美元计算，1998 年的人均 GDP 是

annual market value of all final goods and services produced within a country. Per-capita GDP is simply GDP divided by total population. Measured in 2000 dollars, it was $ 32,833 in 1998 and $ 37,832 in 2006. The real value of goods and services bought by Americans in 2006 was thus about 15 percent higher than it was in 1998. In purely economic terms, does that mean we were roughly 15 percent better off in 2006?

Not necessarily. To measure changes in the standard of living over time, it is necessary to adjust for inflation. But as conservatives stress, traditional inflation adjustments may overstate actual inflation because they fail to account adequately for quality improvements. For example, although the current Honda Civic, a compact① car, is about the same size as the company's midsize Accord from 1998, it is in almost every respect far superior and sells for only slightly more than the earlier Accord. Because inflation adjustments for auto prices are based on changes for corresponding models, the result is to overstate increases in ownership costs — thereby causing per-capita GDP to understate the corresponding increases in our standard of living. Quality changes are not always positive, by the way. If you had a question about your health insurance in 1998, you could talk to a real person; today, you may find yourself in an endless phone loop②. On balance, however, most consumers would probably prefer today's overall menu of goods and services in the economy

---

① compact [ˈkɔmpækt] *adj.* 紧凑的,简洁的

② loop [luːp] *n.*(线、带等绕成的)圈,环,线圈

33 833美元，2006年的人均GDP是37 832美元。美国人在2006年生产的总产品和服务比1998年高出15个百分点。就纯粹的经济状况而言，我们在2006年富了15%吗?

未必是这样。测量生活水平的变化有必要调节通货膨胀。但是，保守派指出，传统的通货膨胀调节方法夸大了实际通货，因为这样做不能充分解释质量的提高。比如，尽管目前经济适用型轿车——本田思域从1998年起，一直和本田公司的中型雅阁尺码一样。因为对汽车价格的通货调节是以车型的变化为基础的，导致的结果就是夸大车主的拥有成本——因此，使人均GDP低估了我们生活质量的相应提高。顺便提一下，质量的变化不总都是向好的方向变。如果你对1998年的健康保险有疑问，你可以说给一个真实的人。今天，你会发现自己在一个没完没了的电话圈套中。总之，大部分的消费者可能更乐意将今天的总产品和服务菜单换成10年前的。

如果在价格不规律上涨时，人们重新调整他们的消费模式，通货调节就可能会将人们进一步引入误区。当牛肉的价格涨幅是鸡肉的两倍时，人们通常会少吃牛肉，多吃鸡肉。传统的通货测量没有充分考虑通货调节——再一次引起了GDP的增长滞后于生活水平的

to that of a decade ago.

Inflation adjustments may introduce further bias if people rearrange their spending patterns when prices rise unevenly. When beef prices rise twice as fast as chicken prices, people typically eat less beef and more chicken. Traditional inflation measures fail to take such adjustments fully into account — again, causing per-capita GDP growth to understate increases in the standard of living. Liberals, for their part, have long objected that many expenditures included in GDP reflect reductions, not increases, in our standard of living. When crime rates increase, people spend more on burglar alarms, purchases that clearly do not signal improved living standards. A similar objection applies when tasks once performed at home are now more often bought in the marketplace — as when time-pressed parents substitute meals at fast-food restaurants for home-cooked meals.

The bias that results from the inclusion of such expenditures in GDP works in the opposite direction from the bias caused by inaccurate inflation adjustment. For all anyone knows, the two distortions may roughly offset each other. But there is a much bigger problem, one that challenges the very foundation of the presumed link between per-capita GDP and economic welfare. That's the assumption, traditional in economic models, that absolute income levels are the primary determinant of individual well-being. This assumption is contradicted by consistent survey findings that when everyone's income grows at about the same rate, average levels of happiness remain the same. Yet at any given

提高。自由主义者一直反对很多指数，包括GDP反映了生活水平的缩减而不是增加。犯罪率上升时，人们在防盗门铃和其他不能清楚地反映生活水平提高的采购方面花的钱会增加。当人们将以前在家干的活经常拿到市场上请人干时，当时间有限的父母用快餐店的食品代替家里做的饭的时候，同样的反对观点也适用。

将这些支出都包括在GDP内产生的偏差就会与不准确的经济调节导致的偏差背道而驰。大家都知道，这两个方向大体上可以相互抵消。但是还有一个更大的问题，一个挑战了人均GDP与经济福利之间那条假定的纽带存在的根基问题。那就是在经济模式中一个很传统的假设，绝对收入水平是个人幸福的主要决定因素。但是这个假设被调查结果一致否定，当人们的收入以同样的比率增长的时候，平均幸福水平保持不变。因而，在任何既定时刻，这个模式都是富人一般来说比穷人幸福。这些发现整体上说明相对收入是一个更好的幸福预言者。

“二战”后的30年间，幸福与收入分布之间的关系不是个大的争论点，因为各个收入群体的收入是以相同的比率增长的。从20世纪70年代中期开始，收入增长几乎被完全限制在高收入群体中。GDP的变化仅跟踪了平均收入变化，对这种改变的影响保持完全沉

moment, the pattern is that wealthy people are happier, on average, than poor people. Together, these findings suggest that relative income is a much better predictor of well-being than absolute income.

In the three decades after World War II, the relationship between well-being and income distribution was not a big issue, because incomes were growing at about the same rate for all income groups. Since the mid-1970s, however, income growth has been confined almost entirely to top earners. Changes in per-capita GDP, which track only changes in average income, are completely silent about the effects of this shift. When measuring the economic welfare of the typical family, the natural focus is on median①, or 50th percentile, family earnings. Per-capita GDP has grown by more than 85 percent since 1973, while median family earnings have grown by less than one-fifth that amount. Changing patterns of income growth have thus caused per-capita GDP growth to vastly overstate the increase in the typical family's standard of living during the past three decades.

Some economists have advanced an even stronger claim — that there is no link, at least in developed countries, between absolute spending and well-being. Recent work suggests that this is especially true for spending categories in which the link between well-being and relative consumption is strongest. For instance, when the rich spend more on larger mansions or more elaborate coming-of-age parties for their

① median [ˈmiːdjən] *n.* 中位数

默。当测量一个典型家庭的经济福利时，很自然地采用中间数，或50% 的家庭的收入。人均 GDP 从 1973 年开始，上涨了 85%。但是中等家庭的收入总量增长了不到 1/5。因此，由收入增长的变化模式引起了人均 GDP 增长夸大了过去 30 年间典型家庭的生活水平的提高。

一些经济学家则更强烈地声明——绝对消费和幸福没有联系，至少是在发达国家。最近的研究表明，在消费项目上更是这样，幸福与相对消费在消费类别中的联系更紧密。例如，当富人将更多的钱花在买大房子或提高孩子的生日聚会上，明显的效果是仅重新定义了什么是富足。证据同样表明，较高的消费在最大程度上刺激了消费连锁反应，这迫使中等收入的家庭以相互抵消的方式消费。如果人们都在面试服装上花的钱多一些，结果还是像以前一样，同样的求职者获得同样的工作。在其他消费项目上，较高的绝对收入水平明显提高幸福，即使在最富裕的国家。经济学家本杰明·弗里德曼发现 GDP 的较高增长率是和社会对于经济弱势群体的包容和支持水平的提高联系在一起的。富裕的国家通常比贫穷的国家环境清洁，国民健康水平高。

人均 GDP 是一个有缺憾的经济福利指数已不是什么新闻。最近

children, the apparent effect is merely to redefine what counts as adequate. Evidence also suggests that higher spending at the top instigates① expenditure cascades② that pressure middle-income families to spend in mutually offsetting ways. Thus, when all spend more on interview suits, the same jobs go to the same applicants as before. Yet in many other categories, greater levels of absolute income clearly promote well-being, even in the richest societies. The economist Benjamin Friedman has found that higher rates of GDP growth are associated with increased levels of social tolerance and public support for the economically disadvantaged. Richer countries also typically have cleaner environments and healthier populations than their poorer counterparts.

THAT per-capita GDP is an imperfect index of economic welfare is not news. The lesson of recent work is that its weaknesses are more serious than we previously realized. And it is an especially uninformative metric when income inequality has been rising sharply, as it has been in recent decades. A society that aspires to improve needs a better measure of what counts as progress.

(1,050 words)

① instigate [ˈinstigeit] *v.* 煽动,唆使
② cascade [kæsˈkeid] *n.* 层叠;喷流

的研究表明，它的缺点比我们意识到的还要严重。就像在近几十年中，当收入差距大幅拉大时，它尤其是个不能反映信息的标准。一个渴求进步的社会需要能够反映进步的更好的量度标准。

知识链接

GDP 国内生产总值(gross domestic product)指在一定时期内(一个季度或一年)，一个国家或地区的经济中所生产出的全部最终产品和劳务的价值，常被公认为是衡量国家经济状况的最佳指标。它不但可反映一个国家的经济表现，还可以反映一国的国力与财富。

题 记

西方主流发展模式的中心由于国民幸福总值悄无声息的入侵而受到了强烈的震撼。金钱买不到幸福，这个事实并不是对资本主义的控诉。用诚实、公正和仁慈的价值观适当维系的体制构成了国民幸福总值的重要因素。研究表明，一个人能挣多少钱在很大程度上与是否幸福并不相关，因为人们真正渴望的是成功，而不是金钱。而成功在各个不同方面的平衡，如家庭生活、精神生活和友谊，这些都是金钱无法衡量的。这些价值体系建立了公民社会体系中人与人之间相互联系的纽带，帮我们避免道德价值观上的错误。当国民幸福总值取代国民生产总值之时，国民幸福总值也构成了一次经济学意义上的“范式转移”，就像从中世纪的地心说转移到哥白尼的日心说。

Key Ingredient in Our Gross National Happiness

You've heard it a thousand times: Money doesn't buy happiness. Yet in spite of this axiom①, people throughout history have tried mightily to accumulate riches. Are we suffering from some sort of collective delusion, or is it possible that money truly does buy happiness?

Let's take the global view first. Compare Mexico and France. In Mexico, most people live above the level of subsistence, but the average purchasing power is only about a third what it is in France. And yet Mexicans, in aggregate, are happier than the French. In Mexico, 63 percent of adults said they were very happy or completely happy. In France, only 35 percent gave one of these responses. Two psychologists interviewed 22 major lottery winners and found that the joy of sudden wealth wore off in a few months. They had a harder time than others enjoying life's prosaic② pleasures: watching television, shopping,

① axiom['æksiəm] *n.* 公理,格言
② prosaic[prəu'zeiik] *a.* 单调的,无趣的

国民幸福总值的重要因素

也许你已经听过一千遍了：金钱买不到幸福。尽管这是一条真理，但自有史记载以来，人们总在尽全力积聚财富。这到底是我们集体的某种错觉，还是金钱真的可能买到幸福？

首先，让我们用全球视野对墨西哥和法国做一个比较。在墨西哥，大多数人的生活水平仅能够维持生存，平均购买力差不多只有法国的三分之一。但墨西哥人总体要比法国人幸福。在墨西哥，63% 的成年人说他们非常幸福或完全幸福。在法国，仅有 35% 的人给出这样的回答。两位心理学家访问了 22 个中奖彩民，发现天降横财的喜悦会在几个月后逐渐消失。他们在享受生活的平凡乐趣时比其他人更不开心，如电视、购物、与朋友聊天等。引起这种现象的原因是人们倾向于从心理上很快地适应自己的环境，包括他们的财政状况。经济学家们称之为“享乐适应征”。

有研究表明，我们能挣多少钱在很大程度上与我们是否幸福并不相关，我们比其他人多挣多少才是关键。在一项哈佛大学

talking with friends, and so forth. The reason for this phenomenon is that humans tend to adapt psychologically to their circumstances — including their monetary ones — quickly. Economists call this the "hedonic treadmill①".

Some research appears to suggest that how much money we make is largely irrelevant to our happiness; it's how much more we make than others that matters. In one study involving faculty, staff, and students at Harvard, participants were asked to choose between earning $ 50,000 per year while everyone else made $ 25,000, or earning $ 100,000 per year while others made $ 200,000. It was stipulated② that prices would be the same in both cases, so a higher salary really meant being able to own a nicer home or buy a nicer car. But that didn't matter much: 56 percent chose the first option, hypothetically③ forgoing $ 50,000 per year simply to feel richer. Do we really care more about one-upmanship than material comforts? Hardly. What the data tell us is that richer people are happier than poorer people because they feel successful in their lives. And it is success — not money — that we really crave.

Financial status is one way we often measure our success. There is nothing strange about this; we measure things indirectly all the time. What scholars often portray as an ignoble④ tendency — acquiring more than

① hedonic treadmill 享乐适应症
② stipulate[ˈstipjuleit] *v.* 规定,明定
③ hypothetically[haipəuˈθetikəli] *ad.* 假设地,假想地
④ ignoble[igˈnəubl] *a.* 卑贱的,不光彩的

的教师、员工和学生参与的调查中，参与者被要求对下列问题做出选择：你是希望自己每年挣 5 万美元而别人只挣 2.5 万美元，还是自己挣 10 万美元而别人挣 20 万美元。由于调查规定了两种情况下相同的物价水平，因此较高的薪水实际上意味着可能拥有更好的房子或购买更好的车。但是，这个关系并不是很大：56% 的参与者选择了第一种情况，假想自己每年放弃 5 万美元但可以感觉更富有。与物质享受相比，我们真的更关注是否高人一等吗？很难就此下定论。这个数据告诉我们，较富有的人比较贫穷的人更幸福，因为他们感觉自己的生活更成功。我们真正渴望的是成功，而不是金钱。

经济地位是我们经常用来衡量成功与否的一种方法。这没有什么可奇怪的，因为我们总是间接地衡量事物。学者们经常将比别人获得更多的想法描述成不光彩的心理趋势，但它的确是驱使我们努力创造更多价值的证据。这是一种美德而不是恶行。它也会带给我们快乐，这个事实就是巨大的幸福。金钱是衡量成功的一种手段，而且是很方便的一种。但是，这个事实还有阴暗的一面：人们常常会忘记，金钱只是一种手段。有些人为了赚钱而赚钱，忘记了真正带给我们幸福的事物。毫无疑问，你肯定遇到过这样的人，他们陷入物质主义和忧愁构成的不满怪圈，不能自拔。他们混淆了金

others — is really evidence that we are driven to create value. This is a virtue, not a vice. The fact that it also brings us happiness is a tremendous blessing. Money is a measure of success, and a handy one at that. But there is a dark side to this fact: People tend to forget that money is only a measure. Some people focus on money for its own sake, forgetting what really brings the happiness. No doubt you've met people who appear to be trapped in an unsatisfying cycle of materialism and unhappiness. They confuse money for what it is supposed to measure and thereby maximize the wrong thing. Among other things, they leave out of the equation all of the kinds of success — in our family lives, in our spiritual lives, in our friendships — that money does not measure. And even their work choices reflect the sad mistake of forgoing what they love doing for what brings in the most monetary compensation. The evidence on happiness is clear that we should avoid the measurement error of materialism.

Some believe market capitalism is to blame, and what they advocate is: Tax away our incomes at very high rates so that money and success were no longer so highly correlated. Then, that money, if we still bothered to earn it, could be spent on public goods and services instead of big houses and other ostentatious displays of our success. We would be happier if we were forced out of the capitalistic consumers, arms race that we have (literally) bought into. And as a bonus, we could enjoy all the good things the government would give us. Simple, it seems — but misguided. Although consumerism does not buy happiness, government spending does not, either. On the contrary, it makes us less happy in

钱以及金钱所衡量的东西，并且把这种错误不断放大。除了其他因素，他们还忽略了成功在各个不同方面的平衡，如我们的家庭生活、我们的精神生活、我们的友谊等，都是金钱无法衡量的。他们的工作选择也反映了这种可悲的错误——放弃他们喜欢做的事情、选择能够带来金钱补偿最大化的工作。幸福的证据很明显：我们应该避免物质主义的衡量错误。

有人认为，市场资本主义应该受到指责，他们提倡的是：尽量对收入高者征税，从而使金钱与成功的关系不再那么密切。那么，如果我们仍然为挣钱感到烦恼，就可以把钱花在公共商品和服务上，而不是花在购买大房子或是其他炫耀我们成功的陈列品上。如果我们被迫退出我们已经造成的（表面如此）资本主义消费者的军备竞赛时，就会更加快乐。作为奖励，我们可以享受政府给予我们的所有的美好事物。这看似简单，其实是一种误导。虽然消费主义不能买到幸福，但政府的支出也不能买到幸福。相反，它会使我们从总体上更加不幸福。

研究显示，较高的政府开支迫使平均幸福水平下降而不是上升。经常以美元回报成功的市场体系可以造就一种趋势，把成功本身与金钱相混淆。但是，允许政府更多地拿走我们辛苦赚来的钱并不能改善这种状况。相反，如果政府试图通过税收和公共支

general.

Research shows that higher government spending turns out to be pushing average happiness down, not up. The market system, which often rewards success with dollars, can create the tendency to confuse success itself with money. But allowing the government to take more of our hard-earned money will not fix this; on the contrary, government would only make things worse for us if it tried to adjust our values through taxation and public spending. The moral confusion of materialism is one best left to ourselves, our families, our communities, and our faiths to resolve. Alexis de Tocqueville wrote in his 1835 classic "Democracy in America" about the tendency toward "excessive individualism" in an atomistic American society. Tocqueville noted, however, that the remedy lay not in reordering the American system, but in the institutions of civil society: families, churches, charities, and friendships, which are the connective tissue between people that help us avoid errors in our values. In other words, markets are not enough — we need morality as well, and the institutions that make it possible to express this morality.

Free markets allow us to live the way we want — giving most people maximum buying power and allowing citizens to find jobs that match their skills and passions. How we use this power and freedom is up to us, and depends on our values: We can make decisions that lead to happiness or make us miserable. But to weaken free market capitalism because it does not bring happiness directly would be senseless: It would be like throwing out your computer because it didn't make your coffee. The fact that some

出来调整我们的价值标准，只会把情况弄得更糟。物质主义的道德混淆最好留给我们自己、我们的家庭、我们的社区以及我们的信仰来解决。1835 年，亚历克西斯·托克维尔在他的经典著作《美国的民主》中写道，在原子论的美国社会，有一种“过度的个人主义”倾向。然而，托克维尔强调，补救措施不在于重新安排美国制度，而是建立公民社会体系，即家庭、教会、慈善事业和友情这些人与人之间相互联系的纽带，他们可以帮助我们避免价值观上的错误。换言之，仅有市场不够，我们还需要道德，需要能够体现道德的制度。

自由市场允许我们按我们想要的方式生活，给予大多数人最大化的购买力，允许居民找到与他们的技能和兴趣相一致的工作。我们如何使用这些权力和自由取决于我们自己，依赖于我们的价值观：我们做出的决定可以带我们走向幸福，也可以让我们变得悲惨。但是因为不能直接带给我们幸福就削弱自由市场资本主义，这种做法毫无意义：这就像因为不能给你准备咖啡，你就将电脑扔掉一样。有些身患疾病、或残疾、或受到其他挑战的人在自由市场体系中很难养活自己，这个事实并不表明我们的体制不健全，而是说明我们的道德观出了差错。在一个道德社会中，这些人需要得到我们其他人某种方式的帮助，维护尊严和避免依赖。

sick or disabled or otherwise-challenged people struggle to provide for themselves in a free-market system does not mean there is something wrong with our system — it means there is something wrong with our morals. In a moral society, these people should be aided by the rest of us in a way that preserves dignity and avoids dependence.

The fact that money doesn't buy happiness is no indictment① of capitalism. On the contrary, we know success is vital to happiness. The institution, moored in proper values of honesty, fairness, and charity, is a key ingredient in our gross national happiness.

(1,046 words)

① indictment[in'daitmənt] *n.* 起诉,控告

金钱买不到幸福，这个事实并不是对资本主义的控诉。相反，我们都知道成功对于幸福而言至关重要。用诚实、公正和仁慈的价值观适当维系的体制才是我们国民幸福总值的重要因素。

知识链接

Gross National Happiness 在国际社会，衡量一个人的幸福快乐的标准叫国民幸福总值(Gross National Happiness，or GNH)，或者称作国民幸福指数。幸福指数是衡量人们对自身生存和发展状况的感受和体验，即人们幸福感的一种指数。国民幸福总值由四大支柱组成：社会经济均衡发展、保护自然环境、坚持传统文化和实行良政。

题　记

文明与文化是人类世界的第二空气，经济则是文明与文化的空气。当社会中的每个人每时每刻都在从事经济活动之时，理财观念则潜移默化地贯穿于人类行为的始终。如果说成年人应该学会怎样理财，那么，对于孩子来说，树立正确的金钱观，学会合理地支配金钱则显得更为重要。理财的五大黄金法则既是人们从小必须树立理财观念，也是以后从事经济活动的基础。“省一文则赚一文”宣扬了一种勤俭节约的传统；“坚持预算”是一场关于金钱价值观的谈话；“了解利息的威力”传授了基本的投资理念；“远离债务”彰显了建立良好的信用记录的重要性；“回馈社会”倡导的是一份社会责任。一个又一个的百万富翁就在此“潜移默化”中诞生。

Exerting a Subtle Influence on Financial Planning

It's never too early to start teaching your kids about money. Toddlers[①] can be introduced to the value of money using toy piggy banks and cash registers, while older kids can learn to manage cash and pretend to be real estate moguls[②] by playing Monopoly. To get a taste of trading stocks and mutual funds, there are online games and contests, as well as investment clubs. And more importantly, high schools and colleges around the country are now offering personal finance courses, with some making the class a requirement before graduation.

The first step for parents, say financial planners, is to start talking about money matters at home. "Having conversations about money at a young age lays a good foundation," says Phyllis Silverman, vice-president and senior trust advisor at PNC Financial Services in Pittsburgh. "That's going to create the attitudes and lay the foundation for their

---

① toddler[ˈtɔdlə] *n.* 小孩

② mogul[ˈməugl] *n.* 大人物,巨头,大亨

理财概念的潜移默化

教孩子如何理财永远不会太早。初学走路的孩子可以告诉他们玩具储蓄罐和收银机存钱的价值；大一点的孩子则可以通过玩棋牌游戏学习管理钱财和模仿地产大亨。如果要体验交易股票和共同基金，可以尝试网络游戏和竞赛，以及投资俱乐部。最重要的是，全国各地的高中和大学现在提供一些个人理财方面的课程，有些学校甚至将其定为毕业前的必修课。

理财顾问指出，对父母来说，第一步是在家里开始谈论理财事务，匹兹堡 PNC 金融服务集团的高级顾问和副主席菲利斯·西尔弗曼认为，“小时候讨论理财可以打下良好的基础。这样才能构建理财概念，为他们今后的行动打下基础”。纽约花园城市 CJM 财政管理总裁和创始人查尔斯·马西莫表示，他已经雇佣了一位心理学家，为富有的客户建立一种适当的方式，以便他们和孩子交流，因为很多父母担心，孩子对财富的认识会造成他们的满足感。他说：“他们担心，如果孩子知道将以这种方式拥有财富，就会变懒，没有

future actions." One planner, Charles Massimo, president and founder of CJM Fiscal Management in Garden City, N.Y., says he has hired a psychologist to establish a proper way for his wealthy clients to communicate with their kids, because many parents worry the knowledge of their wealth will create complacency①. "They worry their kids will be lazy and not motivated if they know they'll have money coming their way," he says.

This Five for the Money offers some golden rules about money to pass along to your children. With the right lessons and planning, your kids, as they grow older, may be able to avoid money traps like getting deep in debt from those alluring② but deceptive credit card offers — and embrace sound strategies as they save for big purchases such as graduate school, car, and a home.

1. A penny saved is a penny earned.

Parents can start teaching kids about earning money as early as elementary school, Silverman says. Set a weekly or monthly allowance for chores done around the house, and offer extra for helping neighbors and performing other tasks. "Allowance should not be seen as an entitlement; it should teach responsibility," Silverman says. Then show your kids how to split their earnings into four money jars: for saving, spending, giving, and taxes. While younger children may not necessarily owe Uncle

① complacency[kəmˈpleisənsi] *n.* 自满,自得
② alluring[ˈəljuəriŋ] *adj.* 诱惑的,迷人的

动力。"

"五种理财原则"提供了一些理财金箴，可以传授给你的孩子。伴随孩子的成长，对他们进行正确的教导和规划，也许能够帮助他们避免掉入金钱的陷阱，如诱人但欺骗性的信用卡提供的越来越深的债务。接受良好的策略使他们可以省钱做大买卖，如读研究生、购车和买房等。

1. 省一文则赚一文。

西尔弗曼认为，父母可以早在孩子的小学阶段就开始教他们挣钱。在家里设置一份每周或每月做家务的津贴，并提供一份帮助邻居和完成其他任务的额外津贴。西尔弗曼说："补贴不应被视为一种权利，它应该教会一份责任。"然后，告诉孩子们如何将他们赚的钱分成四个钱罐子：储蓄、开销、赠与和完税。虽然年幼的儿童没有必要将收入的一部分交给山姆大叔，但提高税款意识是有益的。她强调了留出税收资金的重要性："当孩子们长大和开始接触实际工作时，他们会发现，他们赚的钱和能带回家的钱风马牛不相及。"

2. 坚持预算。

马里兰州哥伦比亚的巴尔的摩华盛顿财务顾问罗伯特·瓦西列夫斯基说，把你每月的账单给孩子们看，如汽车付款、房屋按

Sam a portion of their earnings, an awareness of taxes can be useful. "As they get older and get into the workforce, they'll find that what they earn and take home are two different things," she says of the importance of setting aside tax funds.

2. Stick to the budget.

Show your kids your monthly bills such as car payments, mortgage, and utilities, says Robert Wasilewski, a financial advisor at Baltimore Washington Financial Advisors in Columbia, Md. This will not only teach them about your family's cost of living, but also get them involved in the process. "Teaching people about money is a lot like poker," he says. "No one will play until their money is in the pot." Make a list of wants vs. needs with your kids. When it comes to spending, parents need to ask why their kid needs something — or if they just want it. "It's a conversation about values," Silverman explains. Granted, this list will change as teenagers start driving and working part-time, and have busier social lives. They need to learn how to budget their monthly earnings to cover expenses.

3. Learn the power of interest.

Take your child to a bank and open an account that earns interest. Let the child decide how much to put in and let him or her calculate the interest the account is earning over time. Or, rather than hand kids cash to spend each week, parents can put a set amount in the bank account. In a survey, PNC found that 63% of parents set up a banking or investment account, but only about 21% of teens put money into the account or

揭和公共开支。这样做不仅教会了他们如何处理家庭生活开销，而且还让他们参与了这一进程。他声称："教人理财就像打扑克下赌注。只有涉及一大笔钱时，才有人玩这个游戏。"和孩子一起把短缺与需求列张表。涉及开销时，父母要问孩子为什么需要，或者只是想得到它。西尔弗曼解释道："这是一场关于价值观的谈话。"当然，随着青少年开始打零工、参与较繁忙的社会生活，这张清单还会改变。他们需要学习如何预算月收入以支付开支。

3. 了解利息的威力。

把孩子带到银行，开账户赚利息。让孩子自己决定存多少、让他/她计算账户到时候可以赚取的利息。或者，父母可以将一笔钱存入银行账户，而不是每周给孩子零花钱。太平洋邻里协会在一项调查中发现，63%的父母设立了银行账户或投资账户，但仅有21%的孩子将钱存入账户或者投资。

谈到投资，孩子们应该了解如何拥有不同种类并可以在多年之后增值的股票和基金。马西莫说，他的富有客户们建立了投资俱乐部，并让他们的孩子选择三个或四个朋友加入，向他们传授基本的投资理念。瓦西列夫斯基认为，有些在线股市游戏教授年轻人持有短期股票，因为股价往往会上升；重要的教训是不能持有长期股

make investments.

When it comes to investing, children should learn how owning a diverse number of stocks and funds can grow in value over a span of many years. Massimo says his wealthy clients set up investment clubs — and let their kids pick three or four friends to join — to teach them investing basics. Wasilewski thinks that some of the online stock market games teach young people that stocks are a short-term holding and tend to go up, rather than the important lesson that stocks should be owned for the long run and can easily decline. To learn about the economy and personal finance matters, Wasilewski recommends the Federal Reserve's Web site, which also features a Kids Page.

4. Stay out of debt.

Credit card offers with your child's name arrive in the mail sometimes as early as high school. Show your kids your credit card bills and how to pay them off on time to demonstrate how the cost of an item goes up because of the interest charged. And teach children how the bad habit of paying late can put you in a deep financial hole. At the same time, it's important to establish a good credit history, because there will likely be a time when your kids are going to need to borrow money. "The big problem is, young people don't really understand how to get interest to work for them," Wasilewski says.

5. Giving back is the best gift.

票，否则股价容易下跌。要了解经济和个人财务事项，瓦西列夫斯基推荐了联邦储蓄网站，上面也有儿童网页。

4. 远离债务。

有时，带有孩子姓名的信用卡早在他的高中阶段就已经抵达你的邮箱。给孩子展示你的信用卡账单以及如何按时付清，以证明由于收取利息而如何导致商品成本的上升。告诉孩子，不按时付款的坏习惯将如何把你推向财务的黑洞。同时，建立良好的信用记录非常重要，因为孩子也会有需要借钱的时候。瓦西列夫斯基说："年轻人没有真正理解如何让利息为他们工作是个大问题。"

5. 回馈是最好的礼物。

PNC 金融服务集团的西尔弗曼认为，捐款给慈善机构，包括社区的志愿服务，"真正具有让孩子们学习的重要价值"。孩子在很小的时候，可以捐赠衣服和玩具，节假日中经常有各种组织前来收集。根据 PNC 金融服务集团的近期调查，40% 的家长表示，他们鼓励孩子参加社区活动。许多高净值的家庭建立了基金，并让孩子们承担他们想参与的、具有社会责任感的事业。西尔弗曼声称："他们不仅希望讲授馈赠时间的价值，而且还有馈赠金钱时的责任感。"而马西莫说，另一种回馈的方式是教孩子如何投资社会责任股，通常是那些保护生态环境，没有酒精、烟草和枪支的公司，或强调这

Donating① to charities, including volunteering in your community, is "a really important value for children to learn," Silverman at PNC says. At a young age, your kids can donate clothes and toys that are usually collected by organizations around the holidays. According to the recent PNC survey, 40% of parents said they encourage kids to participate in community events. Many high net worth families set up foundations and let their children pick the socially responsible causes they want to get involved with. "They want to teach the value of giving time, but also giving money responsibly," Silverman says. Another way to give back, Massimo says, is teaching kids how to invest in socially responsible stocks — usually companies that are environmentally friendly and don't make alcohol, tobacco, and firearms — or funds that emphasize those kinds of stocks. Whether it's getting, spending, or giving, teaching your children some sound financial principles now should help them to make smarter choices about their money as they grow older.

(1,058 words)

① donate[dəu'neit] *vi.* & *vt.* 捐赠,赠送

种类型股票的基金。无论是获取、支出或给予，随着孩子的长大，现在教给他们一些健全的财务原则将会帮助他们对金钱做出更明智的选择。

知识链接

PNC Financial Services **PNC** 金融服务集团（PNC Financial Services Group Inc.）总部位于匹兹堡，是一家集多种金融服务于一体的金融公司。该公司下设六大系统，除 PNC 银行以外，还有 PNC 顾问公司、PNC 房地产金融和 PNC 信托服务等。PNC 表示匹兹堡总公司（Pittsburgh National Corporation）。

CJM Fiscal Management **CJM** 财政管理公司是美国一家投资理财公司。其理念是帮助富裕的客户建立信心，保持安全和平和的心态，在成熟的投资过程中，达到财富增长的财务目标，在一个非常动荡的世界里提供公正、公平的风险回报。

Uncle Sam “山姆大叔”常被用来代指美国或美国政府，主要在美国、英国，尤其是在新闻界中使用较多。深受美国人民喜爱的“山姆大叔”常以高高的个子、瘦削的面庞，头戴饰星高顶帽，身穿燕尾服和条纹裤的形象示人。美国人还把“山姆大叔”诚实可靠、吃苦耐劳以及爱国主义的精神视为自己民族的骄傲和共有的品质。1961 年，美国国会正式承认“山姆大叔”为美国的民族象征。

题 记

经济学是一门“沉闷的科学”，部分原因是它给说教的乐趣贴上了价格的标签。经济学家们认为，你的钱越多，就一定越幸福。但沮丧的新贵、自杀的总裁、可怜的富豪以及其他并不快乐的有钱人却给出了与经济学家相悖的结论。金钱与它能买来的幸福呈非线性关系，当人们从赤贫阶层摇身变为舒适的中产阶层，会享受到更多的快乐；而从百万富翁进入千万富翁的行列，就不再有乐趣了。在这个世界上，有钱人一直挣扎在财富和幸福的边缘。经济成功不足以衡量幸福，部分原因就是物质主义对幸福的消极影响。这就是为什么尽管近几十年来西方人的收入显著提高，但是人们的幸福感却几乎一直停留在同一水平上。正如所罗门的箴言：“财富多者诱人渔猎，而对于人生，除了徒饱眼福以外又有何用？”

Stumbling on Happiness

All in all, it was probably a mistake to look for the answer to the eternal question — "Does money buy happiness?" — from people who practice what's called the dismal science①. For when economists tackled the question, they started from the observation that when people put something up for sale they try to get as much for it as they can, and when people buy something they try to pay as little for it as they can. Both sides in the transaction, the economists noticed, are therefore behaving as if they would be more satisfied or happier if they wound up receiving more money (the seller) or holding on to more money (the buyer). Hence, more money must be better than less, and the only way more of something can be better than less of it is if it brings you greater contentment. The economists, conclusion: the more money you have, the happier you must be.

Depressed debutantes, suicidal CEOs, miserable magnates② and other unhappy rich folks aren't the only ones giving the lie to this.

① dismal science 沉闷的科学

② magnate[ˈmæɡneit] *n.* 巨头,富豪

在幸福中挣扎

总的来说，从研究被称之为沉闷科学的人中去寻找“金钱能否买来幸福”这一永恒话题的答案，也许是一个错误。因为经济学家处理这一问题时，会从观察人们的交易开始：人们卖东西的时候，会想方设法多赚钱；而当他们买东西的时候，会想方设法少付钱。经济学家们注意到双方在交易中的行为，如果卖者能得到更多的钱、或者买者能留下更多的钱，他们会更满意或更开心。因此，钱多肯定比钱少好，更多的东西如果能给你带来更大的满足，就说明多比少好。经济学家们的结论是：你的钱越多，就一定越幸福。

沮丧的新贵、自杀的总裁、可怜的富豪以及其他并不快乐的有钱人并非是唯一与经济学家的结论相悖的例子。哈佛大学的心理学家丹尼尔·吉伯特在他的畅销书《在幸福中挣扎》中写道：“心理学家们花费了几十年时间研究财富和幸福的关系，他们从总体上得出了这样一个结论：在从一贫如洗到中产阶级的转变过程中，财富的增加会使幸福感相应增加，但之后，财富继续增长带来的快乐少之

"Psychologists have spent decades studying the relation between wealth and happiness," writes Harvard University psychologist Daniel Gilbert in his best-selling "Stumbling on Happiness, "and they have generally concluded that wealth increases human happiness when it lifts people out of abject poverty① and into the middle class but that it does little to increase happiness thereafter."

That flies in the face of② intuition, not to mention economic theory. According to standard economics, the most important commodity you can buy with additional wealth is choice. If you have $20 in your pocket, you can decide between steak and peanut butter for dinner, but if you have only $1 you'd better hope you already have a jar of jelly at home. Additional wealth also lets you satisfy additional needs and wants, and the more of those you satisfy the happier you are supposed to be.

The trouble is, choice is not all it's cracked up③ to be. Studies show that people like selecting from among maybe half a dozen kinds of pasta at the grocery store but find 27 choices overwhelming, leaving them chronically on edge that they could have chosen a better one than they did. And wants, which are nice to be able to afford, have a bad habit of becoming needs (iPad, anyone?), of which an advertising- and media-saturated culture create endless numbers. Satisfying needs brings less emotional well-being than satisfying wants.

---

① abject poverty 赤贫，一贫如洗
② fly in the face of 公然违抗
③ crack up 吹捧

又少。”

不考虑经济理论，这一结论显然与直觉不一致。根据标准经济学，你用额外财富购买的最重要的商品是选择。如果你口袋里有20美元，你就餐时可以选择吃牛排或是花生酱；但如果你只有1美元，你会希望如果家里有一罐果冻就谢天谢地了。额外的财富也会满足你额外的需要和贫困，你的满足感越强烈，理所当然地会感到更幸福。

问题是选择并不像它被吹捧的那么好。研究显示，人们上杂货店喜欢在6种意大利面之间做出选择，如果有27种选择会让人不知所措，使他们长期紧张不安，相比已经做出的选择，他们本可以做得更好。很有可能承受的欲望，有成为需要的坏习惯（有人想要苹果平板电脑吗？），广告和媒体渗透的文化创造了无止境的数字。人们觉得满足需要较之满足欲望的幸福感更少。

人们对自己的生活满意程度究竟感觉如何？全球范围内的调查充分表明，金钱与它能买来的幸福呈非线性关系，当人们从赤贫阶层摇身变为舒适的中产阶层，会享受到更多的快乐，而从百万富翁进入千万富翁的行列，就不再有乐趣了。在一个有代表性的调查中，人们被要求对他们的快乐感或幸福感按1至7级打分，1代表“对我的生活完全不满意”，7代表“完全满意”。那些对此问题作

The nonlinear nature of how much happiness money can buy — lots more happiness when it moves you out of penury① and into middle-class comfort, hardly any more when it lifts you from millionaire to multimillionaire — comes through clearly in global surveys that ask people how content they feel with their lives. In a typical survey people are asked to rank their sense of well-being or happiness on a scale of 1 to 7, where 1 means "not at all satisfied with my life" and 7 means "completely satisfied." Of the American multimillionaires who responded, the average happiness score was 5. 8. Homeless people in Calcutta came in at 2. 9. But before you assume that money does buy happiness after all, consider who else rated themselves around 5. 8: the Inuit of northern Greenland, who do not exactly lead a life of luxury, and the cattle-herding Masai of Kenya, whose dung② huts have no electricity or running water. And proving Gilbert's point about money buying happiness only when it lifts you out of abject poverty, slum dwellers in Calcutta — one economic rung above the homeless — rate themselves at 4. 6.

Studies tracking changes in a population's reported level of happiness over time have also dealt a death blow to the money-buys-happiness claim. Since World War II the gross domestic product per capita has tripled in the United States. But people's sense of well-being, as measured by surveys asking some variation of "Overall, how satisfied are you with your

① penury [ˈpenjuri] *n.* 贫困,贫穷
② dung[dʌŋ] *n.* (家畜的)粪

答的千万富翁的平均幸福指数是5.8。加尔各答那些无家可归的人的平均幸福指数是2.9。然而，在你认为金钱确实能买来幸福之前，考虑一下谁还会把自己的幸福指数评为5.8左右：他们是格陵兰岛北部的因纽特人，过着称不上奢侈的生活；他们是以养牛放牧为生的肯尼亚马赛人，住在满是粪便的窝棚里，既没有通电，也没有自来水。加尔各答贫民窟里的居住者，在经济上比无家可归的人稍好，他们认为自己的幸福指数为4.6，这就证明了吉伯特的观点：只有当金钱使人脱离赤贫时，才可以买来快乐。

人们的幸福程度随时间的推移而变化，这项跟踪研究对"金钱购买幸福"这一主张造成了致命打击。"二战"以来，美国的人均国民生产总值增长了三倍。但从对"总体上，你对生活有多满意"这类询问某种变化的调查来看，人们的幸福感几乎没有增长。日本从战后的废墟中爬了起来，经历了人均国内生产总值的飞速增长，但国民幸福指数没有任何变化。根据鹿特丹伊拉兹马斯大学社会心理学家维恩霍夫的调查，战后持续发展的西欧也存在这种现象。

问题的部分原因归结于正在发展的经济，洗衣机之类的昔日奢侈品成为了必需品，新贵们感觉不到他们的祖父母用洗衣机洗熨、突然从洗衣板中解脱出来的那种快乐。他们认为拥有美泰克洗衣机是理所当然的事。吉伯特写道："年收入5万美元的美国人比年收

life?", has barely budged[1]. Japan has had an even more meteoric[2] rise in GDP per capita since its postwar misery, but measures of national happiness have been flat, as they have also been in Western Europe during its long postwar boom, according to social psychologist Ruut Veenhoven of Erasmus University in Rotterdam.

That's partly because in an expanding economy, in which former luxuries such as washing machines become necessities, the newly affluent don't feel the same joy in having a machine do the laundry that their grandparents, suddenly freed from washboards, did. They just take the Maytag for granted. "Americans who earn $50,000 per year are much happier than those who earn $10,000 per year," writes Gilbert, "but Americans who earn $5 million per year are not much happier than those who earn $100,000 per year." Another reason is that an expanding paycheck, especially in an expanding economy, produces expanding aspirations and a sense that there is always one more cool thing out there that you absolutely have to have. "Economic success falls short as a measure of well-being, in part because materialism can negatively influence well-being," Diener and Seligman conclude.

If money doesn't buy happiness, what does? Grandma was right when she told you to value health and friends, not money and stuff. Or as Diener and Seligman put it, once your basic needs are met "differences

---

① budge [bʌdʒ] *v.* 移动

② meteoric[miːti'ɔrik] *adj.* 疾速的,辉煌而短暂的

入1万美元的美国人更快乐；但年收入500万美元的美国人不一定会比年收入10万美元的美国人更快乐。”另一个原因是，不断增长的薪水、特别是不断增长的经济，使人产生膨胀的欲望，觉得总有一个更酷的东西在那儿，你绝对要拥有它。迪纳尔和塞利格曼由此得出结论：“经济成功不足以衡量幸福，部分原因就是物质主义对幸福的消极影响。”

如果金钱不能买来幸福，什么可以带来幸福呢？奶奶说的没错，她认为值得重视的是健康和朋友，而不是金钱和物质。或者也如迪纳尔和塞利格曼所说，一旦基本需求得到满足，“幸福的差异较少因收入而频繁显现，造成这种区别的因素大多是社会关系和工作享受”。其他研究者补充了这种自我实现感，即生活有意义、属于公民和其他群体、生活在尊重个人权利和法律规则的民主社会的感觉。维恩霍夫认为，如果一个国家期望增加其国民的幸福感，就应该“减少能带来经济增长的投资，在促进良好治理、自由、民主、信任和公共安全政策方面多下工夫”。

如果更多的钱不能买来更多的幸福，那么大多数美国人的行为看起来就显得有点彻头彻尾的疯狂，过去几十年，我们越来越努力地工作，工作时间更长了，工资也膨胀了。但个人不理智的行为对国民经济产生了十分重要的影响，即从未有过的更多的增长和消

in well-being are less frequently due to income, and are more frequently due to factors such as social relationships and enjoyment at work." Other researchers add fulfillment, a sense that life has meaning, belonging to civic and other groups, and living in a democracy that respects individual rights and the rule of law. If a nation wants to increase its population's sense of well-being, says Veenhoven, it should make "less investment in economic growth and more in policies that promote good governance, liberties, democracy, trust and public safety."

If more money doesn't buy more happiness, then the behavior of most Americans looks downright insane, as we work harder and longer, decade after decade, to fatten our Wages. But what is insane for an individual is crucial for a national economy — that is, ever more growth and consumption. Gilbert again: "Economies can blossom and grow only if people are deluded① into believing that the production of wealth will make them happy. Economies thrive when individuals strive, but because individuals will strive only for their own happiness, it is essential that they mistakenly believe that producing and consuming are routes to personal well-being." In other words, if you want to do your part for your country's economy, forget all of the above about money not buying happiness.

(1,094 words)

---

① delude [diˈluːd] *vt.* 迷惑,蛊惑

费。吉伯特再次指出："只有蛊惑人们相信，财富的生产可以使他们幸福，经济状况才会繁荣和增长。个人努力了，经济才可能繁荣，但每个人只是为了自己的幸福而努力工作，实质上，他们错误地认为生产和消费就是通向个人幸福的途径。"换句话说，如果你想为国家的经济做出自己的贡献，就忘掉上面所说的金钱买不来幸福的话吧。

知识链接

dismal science 沉闷的科学。经济学通常被称为"沉闷的科学"，一个原因是经济学不那么讨人喜欢，认真的经济学家常常带来泼冷水似的意见。他们会指出一个表面上看来很吸引人的项目，很可能结局并不那么美妙。另一个原因或许是因为它的真实。经济学探讨的问题以人性的自私为出发点，残忍地剥去伪善的面纱，而这种赤裸的真实让很多人生厌。

Maytag Corporation 美泰克是一家年销售额达 47 亿美元的家用及商用电器企业集团，总部位于美国爱荷华州的牛顿，是北美市场的三大顶级公司之一。美泰克提供种类齐全的洗衣机、干衣机、洗碗机、冰箱等一系列家庭用具，在全球拥有近 2 万名员工。

题　记

城市中，汽车穿梭不息，富翁驾驶的一定是名车吗？商场中，各式品牌目不暇接，富翁一定会购买奢侈品吗？豪华别墅里，住的一定是富人吗？答案是否定的。洛克菲勒在一生中始终保持着沉默寡言、行事低调的风格；比尔·盖茨的生活细节都被掩藏在私邸的围墙和办公室的磨砂玻璃门后面；沃伦·巴菲特以不变应万变的从容与沉静在瞬息万变的股票市场挥斥方遒。富人为了积聚财富长时间地勤奋工作，极少享受电视机前的休闲时光。富人获得和保持富有的方式是通过长期投资他们的金钱而获得杠杆推力，让金钱为他们工作。富人以积极的态度看待财富，对所做的事情充满激情。富人将财富回馈社会，自己也从中享受到了一种快乐。当我们祝福富有者的时候，也揭开了我们自己生命中的无限可能性的潜质，运用已有的才能创造爱心、美好、和平与和谐。

Blessing the Wealthy

What is money? Money is energy and at its most basic, it is a tool that enables you to meet your daily needs. Money has the ability to provoke change for good or for bad therefore it has an emotional attachment.

People have an unconscious reaction to money. Think about it for a moment, let's try a little exercise. I want you to get a piece of paper and a pen and by timing yourself for one minute, write down every word that comes to mind when you think of the word "money". I have done this exercise with people before and here is an example of what the majority of people write down. See if you have written down the same things: greedy; selfish; won it; gamblers; stole it; inherited it; crooked; unethical; drug dealers.

How many of the above did you write down? Generally speaking, people with money or who aspire to become wealthy are often judged harshly①. How do you expect to become wealthy if your mentality around money is negative? Even if you were to win lotto, statistics show that you

---

① harshly[ˈhɑːʃli] *ad.* 粗糙地,粗暴地

祝福富有者

金钱是什么？ 金钱是能量，从最基本的意义上来说，它是你每天生活必不可少的工具。 金钱有能力刺激事物发生或好或坏的变化，所以，它也是一种情感上的依赖。

人们对金钱有一种无意识的反应。 仔细想一想，让我们做个小测试。 拿出纸和笔，在一分钟之内写下你所能想到的关于“金钱”的任何词汇。 以前我曾经给很多人做过这个小测试，下面这些词是大多数人写得最多的。 看看你是否会写同样的词：贪婪、自私、获取、赌徒、偷窃、继承、诈骗、不道德、毒贩。

你写下的词中有多少是和上面一样的呢？ 一般来说，有钱人或者是那些渴望富有的人经常受到严厉的指责。 如果你对于金钱的理解是如此消极，怎么能够变得富有呢？ 有统计表明，即使你赢了彩票，也可能在四到五年内回到现在的经济状况。 怎么会这样呢？如果你的无意识感觉是消极的，怎么期望金钱留在你身边呢？ 因为金钱有能量，它将由消极转向积极，从你的手中流入他人的手中。

would end up in your current financial position within four to five years. Why is this fact? If your unconscious feelings are negative how do you expect money to stick around? As money is energy it will move from negative to positive — out of your hands and into someone else's.

From an early age, we are taught that "money is the root of all evil". I heard a wise man say that the "lack of money is the root of all evil". These negative emotions entrench themselves in our emotional filing cabinets and occasionally they rear their ugly heads as envy or jealousy. These negatives emotions cause us to pass judgment on those who have money. We criticize and are unflattering① in our conclusions of them. Yet we may know very little about them or we fail to understand that their wealth may be the result of working long hours with very little time off. They may work six to seven days per week while others enjoy time relaxing in front of the television or out with friends and family.

Many of the wealthy I know have worked long hours to fast track wealth. I certainly do not want to wait until sixty five years of age to enjoy my wealth. My goal is to achieve a certain level of comfort by the time I am forty. If that means working my butt off② until then, then so be it③. I call it short term pain for long term gain. You can't build wealth by watching television; action is the order of the day. I admire all the hard

① unflattering[ʌnˈflætəriŋ] *a.* 坦率的
② butt off *n.*鼓捣
③ so be it *ad.*好罢(但愿如此)

早些时候，我们受到的教导是“金钱是万恶之源”。我曾听一位智者说过这样一句话，“缺钱是所有罪恶的根源”。这些消极的情绪在我们的情感文件柜中筑起壕沟防护自己，偶尔从背后伸出羡慕或嫉妒的肮脏头颅。我们带着这些负面的情绪判断那些有钱人。我们对他们极尽挑剔，直言不讳地做出结论。其实，我们可能对他们了解极少，或者是我们没有理解，他们的财富可能是长时间工作、极少休息的结果。他们每周可能工作六到七天，而其他人却在电视机前享受休闲时光，或者和朋友、家人外出。

我认识的许多有钱人都是长时间工作，以求快速积聚财富。我当然不想等到65岁时才开始享受我的财富。我的目标是在40岁时达到某种级别。如果这意味着到时一直要辛苦地工作，那就顺其自然吧！我称之为为了长期享受的短期痛苦。看电视不可能积累财富，要靠每天踏踏实实的行动。我钦佩所有勤奋工作的富人，他们成功地达到了自己的目标。坐在马车上，财富不会自动跑过来。

我想强调这种观点，当你对所做的事情充满激情时，努力工作成为了一种乐趣。我喜欢我所做的事情，所以每周工作六至七天是一种享受。我喜欢创造性思维，不按常理出牌。我喜欢教育我的客户，我喜欢写作。我尤其陶醉于和他人分享我的知识，那样他们也能过得更好。

work of the wealthy and successful to achieve their goals. It will not happen automatically while sitting on the coach.

I do have to say at this point that working hard becomes a pleasure when what you do is a passion. I love what I do so working six to seven days per week is a pleasure. I enjoy thinking creatively and outside the square; I enjoy educating my clients and I enjoy my writing. I especially get a buzz out of sharing my knowledge with others so that they may experience a better life.

Let's go back to the exercise on the meaning of money. From a positive perspective, those who completed the exercise had positive things to say: freedom; success; deserving; ethical; grateful; abundant; happiness; power; security. If you had any of these words then you are in the ten percent. Only about ten percent of people in my experience complete this task in a positive way. I find it to be a very interesting and a worthwhile exercise in getting people to clearly understand why they attract or repel money.

The other interesting fact about the wealthy is that many give some of their wealth back regularly. We do the same; each month we financially support three charities. When I was poor, I used to begrudge① giving five dollars to the Salvation Army② as the five dollars would sometimes make the difference between me having one or two meals in that day. I used to

---

① begrudge [bi'grʌdʒ] v. 嫉妒,羡慕

② Salvation Army n.〈基督教〉救世军

让我们回到关于金钱含义的小测验上来。从积极的角度来看，那些完成测试的人同样列出了一些积极的词汇：自由、成功、奖励、伦理的、感激的、富裕的、幸福、权力、安全。如果你写下了以上词汇中的任何一个，那么你就属于百分之十中的一员。在我的这种测验中，只有约百分之十的人以积极的心态完成了测验。我觉得这是一种非常有趣、值得一做的测验，让人们清楚地了解为什么他们渴望或排斥金钱。

另一个关于富人的有趣事实是，许多人定期将财富回馈社会。我们也这样做。我们每月给三家慈善机构捐款。在我贫穷时，给救世军捐5美元都会舍不得，因为5美元有时的区别就是当天吃一顿饭还是两顿饭。我过去常常希望多捐一点，但经济实力不行。一提到金钱和慈善，我觉得我只有回馈社会才能富有，因为我挣的钱越多，回馈社会也就越多，相信我，我要为这个世界做很多贡献。

如果你对金钱的态度是消极的，那么此类想法一出现就要试着去改变。资金紧张时，有时很难尽力地积极思考，但我克服嫉妒情绪有自己的方法，就是想象这是身着华丽服饰、开着豪车站在我面前的人应得的。他们一直在为他们所得到的努力奋斗，所以他们应该拥有一切。不久之后，我发现对他们的良好祝福变得自然而然。

wish I could give more but financially couldn't. When it comes to money and charity, I feel that I owe it to society to be wealthy because the more money I earn, the more I can give back and believe me I have lots I want to do for the world.

If your emotions around money are negative, try to alter your feelings at the time they start to surface. It's sometimes hard when money is tight to try and think positively however the way I overcame the emotion of jealousy was to think of that person standing in front of me with their fancy clothes and nice car as deserving. They have worked hard for what they have achieved and therefore they deserve it. After sometime I found wishing them well came naturally. Now jealousy is an emotion I have not experienced for two decades. Take a moment to consider your emotions around money. Money means different things to everyone. It's what we can do with the money that makes the difference. Try to develop an abundant mentality around money and accept that while some have and other don't, we all have the potential of unlocking unlimited possibilities in our own lives by creating love, beauty, peace and harmony① by using the gifts we have been given.

(929 words)

---

① harmony [ˈhɑːməni] *n.* 协调,和睦

20 年来，嫉妒心理几乎从我的生命中消失了。 花点时间思考你对金钱的情绪。 金钱对每个人都有不同的含义，正是我们用金钱做什么才具有真正的意义。 试着激发自己以丰富的心态去追求金钱，并接受有些人有钱、而另一些人没有钱的现实，我们所有人都具备揭开我们自己生命中的无限可能性的潜质，可以运用已有的才能，创造爱心、美好、和平与和谐。

知识链接

Salvation Army 救世军是一个世界性的基督教慈善组织，有着严格的军事化结构和管理。其宗旨是以基督教为背景，开展教育、扶贫和其他慈善项目，帮助有需要的人提高生活水平，以益于全人类及全社会。救世军成立于 1865 年，总部在英国伦敦，至今分部已遍及全球 100 多个国家。

题　记

“你能够看到的未来有多远，你的事业就能够走多远。”这一简单原则是犹太羊皮卷《塔木德》中的精髓，也是我们同时拥有成功和幸福的指南。在财富的世界里，简单原则作为独特的价值和追求愈来愈显示出其与众不同的魅力：我们应该学会满足于我们已经拥有的财富，并享受简单的好处；不要把自己和金钱绑在一起；把钱当做生活当中很小的一部分，并尽可能少地考虑钱的问题；避免嫉妒有钱人；不要为工作而活着；理解为什么有些人总是贫穷；尽量避免想钱，但也不能无视金钱带来的问题。越简单的理财价值观，涉及的变量关系越少，整体幸福生活指数也会越高。简单理财的魅力在于去芜取菁，分清主次，突出重点，提高生活质量，还我们的内心一片绿洲和安宁。

The Value of Simplicity

It is an often repeated axiom that money cannot buy happiness. While this is certainly true, poverty will not buy happiness either. Some people become very wealthy, yet struggle to enjoy their lives. On the other hand, others manage to go through life with very few money problems simply because they are able to make the most of what they have. Ideally you should try to combine both prosperity and happiness. To do this I recommend the following steps:

1. Learn to Value Simplicity

The aim of life should not be to accumulate as many possessions and as much wealth as possible. We should learn to be content with what we have and appreciate the benefits of simplicity. For example, if we clear out our unnecessary clutter① we will achieve a greater feeling of space and freedom.

2. Do Not Be Attached to Your Money

Does it pain you to spend your own money — even if it is for something useful? Even someone like Bill Gates can feel uncomfortable

---

① clutter [ˈklʌtə] *n.* 喧嚣,混乱,零乱

简单的价值

这是一条经常被重复的公理：金钱不能买到幸福。虽然这是理所当然的真理，但贫穷也不可能买到幸福。有些人非常富有，但仍然在挣扎中享受生活。另一方面，有些人能够好好过日子，生活中很少有金钱问题，因为他们能够充分利用已有的资源。理想的是，你应该尝试同时拥有成功和幸福，为此我推荐下列原则：

1. 学习简单的价值

生活的目标不应该只是尽可能地积累大量的物质和财富。我们应该学会满足于我们已经拥有的财富，并享受简单的好处。例如，如果我们理清了不必要的混乱，就会取得更大的空间和自由的感觉。

2. 不要把你和你的金钱绑在一起

你是否会在花自己钱的时候感到心疼，即使是去买有用的东西？即使比尔·盖茨花自己的钱也会感到不舒服。据说他总是乘坐经济舱旅行，因为他认为没有必要花更多的钱坐头等舱。但问题是如果我们始终不愿意花钱，那就完全失去了赚钱的意义。良好的

spending his billions; it is said he used to always travel economy class because he didn't see the need to spend more money on first class. The problem with this, however, is that if we are always reluctant to spend money we miss the whole point of earning it. A good attitude is to see money as a circular flow — that is, spending money enables more to come into our lives. It is not like a big dam where we just try to hold onto it all. We need to let the money out by spending on useful and necessary things. It is no good having a stockpile of water unless we use it to generate power; similarly it is no use accumulating large savings if we feel miserable spending it.

3. Minimize Money Worries

We will be happiest if we can make money a small part of our lives, and think about money issues as little as possible. To be able to do this we need to avoid creating situations of debt as getting out of debt can be difficult and stressful. Learn to live within your means by avoiding impulsive overspending. If you do need to go into debt, plan ahead and find a loan which is clear and manageable to repay. Try to avoid complicated and risky investment plans; these give you the potential to gain more, but you will also have the potential to lose a lot more. Good financial planning should be simple and well balanced; this means your nerves will not be affected by worrying about the outcome of your investment. It is better to invest and save in something secure so you can forget about it and not worry endlessly.

4. Avoid Jealousy

No matter how much money you have, do you still envy people who

态度是把钱看做一个循环流，即花钱能使我们赚更多的钱。它不像一个大水坝，我们只想守住这一切。我们需要让资金外流，花在有益和必要的事情上。除非我们用水发电，否则就没有必要存水；同样的，如果我们花钱时感到很心痛，那么积累大量的存款也没有意义。

3. 尽量减少对金钱的忧虑

如果我们把钱当做生活当中很小的一部分，并尽可能少地考虑钱的问题，将是最大的幸福。为了能够做到这一点，我们必须避免欠债，因为深陷债务很难摆脱，而且压力很大。学会量入为出，避免冲动的超支。如果确实需要借债，应该提前计划，找一份清楚且易于偿还的贷款。尽量避免复杂并具有风险的投资计划，这些做法可能使你获得更多，但也有可能失去更多。良好的财务规划应简单且合理地平衡，这意味着你的神经将不会因为担忧投资结果而受到影响。最好选择安全的投资和储蓄，这样你就可以忘记它，不会无休止地担心。

4. 避免嫉妒

不管你有多少钱，你仍然会羡慕比你更有钱的人吗？最近有一项调查，询问人们是否愿意拥有一份高于全国平均水平的工资。或者，他们可以选择更高的工资，但这一更高的工资低于平均水平。出乎意外的是，大多数人选择了较低的工资，只要这意味着他们比其他人相对富裕即可。这对我来说没有任何意义。如果其他人比

have more? A recent survey asked people whether they would prefer to have a salary above the national average. Alternatively, they could choose to have a higher salary, but this higher salary would be lower than the average. A surprising amount of people chose to have a lower salary as long as it meant they were relatively better off than the rest of the population. To me this makes no sense. If other people become wealthier than you, that is no reason to be unhappy. If other people are prosperous① that is good; don't feel miserable just because you cannot keep up with the Joneses.

5. Don't Live to Work.

Do you find yourself working overtime in the evenings and at the weekend? If you spend all your time working, you will have no opportunity to spend your earnings. Don't feel guilty for turning extra work down; it is important to give leisure time as high a priority② as work. It is good if we can gain satisfaction from work, but if we only spend time working then our life lacks a proper balance.

6. Understand Why Are Some People Always Poor

I'm sure most people will have good friends who always seem to have money concerns. No matter what happens they always seem to be short of money and they frequently share tales of financial woe. The lack of money makes them unhappy, but they don't know how to change the situation. Giving them money doesn't solve the problem because they continue to

---

① prosperous [ˈprɔspərəs] *adj.* 繁荣的,昌盛的

② priority [praiˈɔriti] *n.*优先,优先权

你富裕，没有理由不高兴。如果其他人很富裕也无可厚非，不要因为你比与自己社会地位相等的人条件差就觉得痛苦。

5. 不要为工作而活着

你有发现自己在晚上和周末加班吗？ 如果你把所有的时间都花在工作上，就没有机会花你赚的钱。 不要因为拒绝额外工作而感到沮丧，休闲和工作同样重要，都要给予优先考虑。如果我们能从工作中获得满足感当然很好，但如果我们只花时间工作，那么我们的生活就缺乏适当的平衡。

6. 理解为什么有些人总是贫穷

我敢肯定，大部分人都有些好朋友，他们总是为钱发愁。 无论发生什么事情，他们似乎总是很缺钱，经常叫嚷经济拮据。 缺钱令他们不开心，但他们却不知道如何改变这种状况。 给他们钱不能解决问题，因为他们会继续做出糟糕的财政决策。 部分问题在于他们的心态，人们对于贫穷容易习以为常，于是部分期待贫穷还会持续下去。 有这种心态就很难吸引金钱进入我们的生活，容易产生自我怜悯和遗憾的感觉。 然而，虽然我们很不幸，但无法改变这种状况。 秘诀就是要试图改变我们面对金钱的习惯和方法。 此外，说服他人采取更好的理财习惯时要小心谨慎，做这种事几乎注定是要失败的。

7. 无知不是幸福

另一种对待钱的态度是尽量避免想钱。 我们会忽略债务、开销

make bad financial decisions. Part of the problem lies in their mindset. It is easy to become accustomed to being poor and then half expecting the poverty to continue. With this mindset, it becomes difficult to attract money into our lives and easy to develop feelings of self-pity and regret. However, while we might be unfortunate it won't do anything to resolve the situation. The secret is to try and change our habits and approach to money. Also, be wary about trying to convert others to better financial habits — it is almost guaranteed to fail.

7. Ignorance is Not Bliss①

Another attitude to money is to try and avoid thinking about it. We ignore the true extent of our debts, spending and leaving unpaid bills. We frequently miss out on moving to better financial deals and make late payments which harm our credit rating. By ignoring money like this, we merely create more serious problems for the future. Also, when we put off dealing with financial problems we carry the problem in the back of our mind. We can get no peace of mind because we permanently have a long list of things to deal with. It is better in these circumstances to promptly deal with things like paying bills and sorting out your accounts — then we can forget about them completely.

(956 words)

① bliss [blis] *n.* 幸福,极乐

和未付账单的真实性。我们经常错过较好的金融交易，还延迟付款，这些做法损害了我们的信用评级。如此这般地无视金钱，只会使未来的问题更严重。此外，当我们拖延处理财政问题时，其实问题已经遗留在脑海中了。由于我们永远有一长串的事情要处理，内心一刻也不得安宁。在这种情况下，最好及时处理付账和整理账户等问题，然后把它们全部忘光。

知识链接

Bill Gates 比尔·盖茨是全球个人计算机软件的领先供应商——微软公司的创始人，他有关个人计算机的远见和洞察力一直是微软公司和软件业界成功的关键。比尔·盖茨很俭朴，出行一向只坐经济客位，哪怕后来成为亿万富翁，也只买最便宜的机票。航空公司只要见到比尔·盖茨，就自动将其升格到头等舱。他心知肚明，更加不买贵的机票。虽然成为全球首富后已改搭商务客位，但比尔·盖茨仍不习惯住总统套房。

题 记

物质财富与精神财富，就像有人说的一半是天使，一半是魔鬼，因为一个用来寄托，一个用来生活。当寄托的美好与现实的生活交织，就会直接导致物质与精神的困惑。伟大的投资家约翰·邓普顿坚信，精神上的富有是整个世界的财富，可以用坚实的精神基础和人性化的原则铺一条通向财富成功的道路。他是世界上最有钱的人之一，他的逆向投资哲学已经成为邓普顿基金集团的投资团队以及许多投资人永恒的财富。但他也是精神最为富有者之一，他已经捐出了自己的大部分财富，他的邓普顿基金，拥有11亿美元的资产，每年抽出6 000万美元作为邓普顿奖金，包括100万美元的世界最大单项奖。他还特别强调：道德准则增加了、而不是减少了投资者的长期收益。通向精神财富的道路并不容易穿越，但约翰·邓普顿却用自己的亲身经历向世人证明，这条路能够带领我们找到生活中真正的宝藏。

The Road Map to Spiritual Wealth

Everyone has his heroes. In my eyes, none living stands larger than 95-year-old Sir John Templeton. Templeton is not just a brilliant man, but a Rhodes Scholar. One of the world's undisputed money masters, magazines have described him as "one of the handful of true investment greats in a field crowded with mediocrity① and bloated② reputations."

Templeton almost single-handedly pioneered the discipline of global equity investing. He believes any investor would be foolish to restrict his investments to his home country. Seek out the world's best investments, he advises, wherever they reside. In the 1950s, for example, he poured shareholders money into the German and Japanese stock markets. With the wounds of WWII still fresh, investing in Japan was about as popular with Americans then as the idea of funding the Taliban today. But as these battered③ economies were gradually rebuilt, his investment returns were substantial. Today he still favors the investment outlook for emerging markets, particularly China.

At the height of the Internet bubble, Templeton sold short dozens of

---

① mediocrity [ˌmiːdiˈɔkriti] *n.* 普通,平凡

② bloated [ˈbləutid] *adj.* 发胀的,肿起的

③ battered [ˈbætəd] *adj.* 打扁了的;弄垮的

通向精神财富的道路

每个人都有自己的英雄。在我的眼中，没有任何活着的人比95岁的约翰·邓普顿爵士更伟大。邓普顿不仅是一个睿智的人，也是罗德岛的一名学者。作为世界上无可置辩的金融大师之一，报纸杂志将他描述为“在平庸和傲慢膨胀的投资领域为数不多的真正伟大的投资家之一”。

邓普顿几乎是单枪匹马地开创了全球股票投资的方法。他确信，任何投资者将其投资限制在本国之内都是愚蠢的行为。他给出的忠告是，不管他们住在哪，都应该在全球范围内寻找最好的投资机会。例如，在20世纪50年代，他将股东的资金大量注入德国和日本的股票市场。由于“二战”的伤口依旧让人记忆犹新，美国人普遍认为，当时投资日本就像今天资助塔利班一样。但是随着这些被压垮了的经济逐渐恢复，他的投资收益相当可观。今天，他依然看好新兴的投资市场，特别是中国市场的前景。

在互联网泡沫的鼎盛时期，邓普森在价格被“锁定”之前短线卖出几十家新兴科技公司的股票，首次公开募股之后就是6个月的冷却周期。他在短短几周内收益超过8 000万美元。他仍然称之为“我有史以来赚得最容易的钱”。约翰·邓普顿知道，什么是真正

young technology companies just before their shares came out of "lock-up," the six-month cooling off period following an IPO. He made over $80 million in a matter of weeks. He still calls it "the easiest money I ever made." John Templeton knows what it means to be a true contrarian①. "To buy when others are despondently② selling and to sell when others are avidly buying requires the greatest fortitude③, and pays the greatest reward." Wise words for those contemplating what to do in today's volatile markets.

At one time, Templeton was one of the world's richest men. But now he has given most of his fortune away. His Templeton Foundation, with assets of more than $1.1 billion, awards over $60 million each year, including the $1 million Templeton Prize, the world's single largest award. In 1987, he was knighted by Queen Elizabeth II for his philanthropic④ efforts, including his endowment of Templeton College, Oxford. Yes, John Templeton has achieved more than most of us can dream of. But his accomplishments are not the only reason he's a personal hero of mine. It's also his philosophy of life. As a young man starting out as a money manager, I idolized⑤ Templeton, devouring his books and lectures. In the process, he revealed a lot more than just successful investment principles.

---

① contrarian [kənˈtrɛəriən] *n.* 做法与一般大众想法相反的投资人(例如:买冷门股票)

② despondently [diˈspɔndəntli] *adv.* 意志消沉地,沮丧地

③ fortitude [ˈfɔːtitjuːd] *n.* 坚忍,刚毅

④ philanthropic [filənˈθrɔpik] *adj.* 慈善的,乐善好施的

⑤ idolize [ˈaidəlaiz] *vt.* 过度崇拜,奉为神圣

的逆向投资。“在他人沮丧地抛售股票时买进，在他人贪婪地买进时抛出，这需要最大的勇气，但也会收获最大的奖励。”在当今动荡的市场，这对那些考虑如何操作的人来说是十分明智的忠告。

邓普顿曾经是世界上最有钱的人之一，但是现在他已经捐出了自己的大部分财富。他的邓普顿基金，拥有11亿美元的资产，每年抽出6 000万美元作为邓普顿奖金，包括100万美元的世界最大单项奖。1987年，由于他乐善好施的行为，包括对牛津大学邓普顿学院的捐建，邓普顿获英国女王伊丽莎白二世册封爵士勋衔。诚然，约翰·邓普顿已经取得了我们大部分人做梦也无法达到的成就。但是他的成就并不是他成为我个人的英雄的唯一原因。我还崇尚他的人生哲学。作为一名刚刚起步的年轻的基金经理，我极端崇拜邓普顿，贪婪地阅读了他的书籍和演讲。在这个阅读的过程中，邓普顿向我们展示了远比成功投资原则强大的魅力。

约翰·邓普顿喜欢说：“追求的幸福会溜走，给出的幸福会回来。”邓普顿坚信，真正的财富不是来自于赚钱，而是来自于实现我们自身之外的目标，不管是锻炼我们的才能，还是将我们的孩子培养成快乐、有用的成人，或者是以某种有意义的方式回馈我们的社会。正如他的书《邓普顿计划》所言，例如，邓普顿引用社会改革家亨利·沃德·比彻的语录：“人死后，没有人说得出他是富有还是贫穷。是人心使一个人变得富有。判断一个人是否富有不是根据他拥有什么，而是根据他是什么样的人来做出决定。”

在全国各地的投资研讨会和咨商会议上，我见到成百上千的个人投资者将这句话铭记在心，并且恪守着这种信念。例如，几年前在圣胡安的一次会议上，我遇到一位年长的绅士，他告诉我作

John Templeton is fond of saying, "Happiness pursued eludes①, happiness given returns." Templeton is a great believer that true wealth doesn't come from making money, but from fulfilling a purpose outside ourselves, whether that's exercising our talents, raising our kids to be happy, productive adults, or contributing to our communities in some meaningful way. As in his book "The Templeton Plan," for instance, Templeton quotes social reformer Henry Ward Beecher, "No man can tell whether he is rich or poor by turning to his ledger②. It is the heart that makes a man rich. He is rich according to what he is, not according to what he has."

At investment seminars and conferences around the country, I'vemet hundreds of individuals who have taken this message to heart — and are busy living it. At a conference in San Juan several years ago, for example, I met an older gentleman who began telling me how much he enjoyed being a member of The Oxford Club. "We'vemade you a few dollars?" I asked. He touched my arm, smiled and said, "Oh, I've been far too fortunate in this life for money to make much difference." What a charming answer.

We sometimes forget that there are two types of riches in this world: material wealth and spiritual wealth. Anything that can be measured in dollars and cents, I call material wealth. Everything else — the love of our families, the health we enjoy, the time we spend doing things we enjoy or working on things that really matter — I call spiritual wealth. I'll still be writing my usual investment commentary here and with The Oxford

---

① elude[iˈluːd] v. 躲避,逃脱

② ledger [ˈledʒə] n. 总账

为一名牛津俱乐部的成员他是多么的高兴。我问道：“我们已经给了您几美元吗？”他拍拍我的肩，笑着说：“哦，我已经太幸运了，在这个为了金钱而活的社会中如此与众不同。”多么睿智的一个答案。

我们有时几乎忘记了这个世界上存在着的两种财富：物质财富和精神财富。任何能够用美元和美分来衡量的财富，我称之为物质财富。其他的东西，即我们家人之间的爱、我们享受的健康、我们做自己喜欢的事时度过的美好时光以及致力于重要的工作，我称之为精神财富。我将继续在这里和牛津俱乐部一起写日常的投资评论。我还打算发送一份免费的半周刊、称为“精神财富”的电子信件。因为两方面的原因，我鼓励大家参与这一活动。

第一个原因是我们所有人都应该解决生活中的大问题。什么是最重要的？我们如何分清轻重缓急？我们如何超越成功到达伟大？当然，我永远相信财政独立是生活最重要的目标之一。它给你自由，做你想做的事，去你想去的地方，和你喜欢的人在一起。金钱使你能够养家糊口，帮助他人，追求自己的知识和艺术爱好，成为社会成员中的精神领袖。然而生活却不只是为了积聚和花费更多的财富。我并不认为成为工作的奴隶、受环境和每月的过度开支压迫的人能够获得真正的快乐。生活中还有许多更重要的事情，而这些正是我们在每周的“精神财富”中要讨论的话题。

我希望你们注册“精神财富”的另外一个原因是，除了我认为你们能够从中获益的事实，我还需要你们的投入。就像我，我敢肯定，你们已经在艰难的道路上吸取了生活中最重要的教训。所以，

Club. But I'm also launching a free, twice-weekly e-letter called Spiritual Wealth. And I encourage you to join me, for two reasons.

The first is that all of us should grapple with the big questions in our lives. What matters most? How do we balance our priorities? How do we move beyond success to significance? Of course, I'll always believe that financial independence is one of life's most important goals. It's what gives you the freedom to do what you want, where you want, with whom you want. Money allows you to provide for your family, help other people, pursue your intellectual and artistic interests, and become an inspiration to members of your community. But life is not about just accumulating and spending more. I don't believe anyone can be truly happy as long as he is a slave to his job, his circumstances, or his monthly overhead. There are plenty of things in life that are more important and those are exactly the subjects we'll discuss in Spiritual Wealth each week.

The other reason I'd like you to sign up for Spiritual Wealth aside from the fact that I think you'll profit from it — is because I need your input. Like me, I'm sure you'velearned many of life's most important lessons the hard way. So whenever I write about a topic you know something about, please don't be reluctant to hit the reply button. In the weeks ahead, feel free to contribute your thoughts, your ideas, and your "two cents worth" whenever you'd like. We can all benefit from your experiences, but perhaps you most of all. As the old Chinese proverb says, "Tell me and I'll forget; show me and I may remember; involve me and I'll understand." So I invite you to give Spiritual Wealth a try. I think you'll profit from it. And — like the best things in life — it's free.

(990 words)

每当我写下一个你所熟悉的话题时，请不要犹豫，点击回复按钮。接下来的几周，只要你们愿意，放心大胆地贡献你的思想、你的观点、你的“两分钱的希望”。我们大家都可以从你的经历中获益，也许你就是所有人中受益最大的那位。正如一句古老的中国谚语：“告诉我，我会忘记；给我看，我会铭记；让我参与，我会理解。”所以，我邀请你到“精神财富”来做一番尝试。我认为你将从中受益。而且，正如生命中最美好的事物一样——它是免费的。

知识链接

Templeton Foundation 美国约翰·邓普顿基金会是一家专门组织国际性科学与宗教对话与研究的机构。邓普顿奖金每年为 100 万英镑(约合 140 万美元)，是世界上最高额的年度奖金。由于邓普顿奖的巨大影响力和与诺贝尔奖数额齐平的奖金，因此该奖也被称为“宗教界的诺贝尔奖”。

题　记

美国钢铁大王安德鲁·卡内基的至理名言是:“在巨富中死去是一种耻辱。”苏格兰头号首富亨特认为,“不想把10亿英镑的财富带入棺材”。这和中国民间“生不带来,死不带走”的财富观有异曲同工之妙。上帝在旧约里面告诉亚伯拉罕,把他全部财富的10%给予上帝,就会受到财富的保佑。这就是吸引法则。于是,出生在20世纪、生活在21世纪的伟大的善男信女们,责无旁贷地实践着吸引法则。唐纳德·特朗普、沃伦·巴菲特和比尔·盖茨等商业人士,几乎将自己的所有家产投入慈善事业。奥普拉·温弗瑞、安吉莉娜·朱丽和玛莎·斯图尔特等强势和有影响力的女性,也都是大慈善家和富有的女人。所以,富人们在积累财富的同时,还应该学会使用财富、学会树立社会形象、学会奉献爱心,让财富在造福自己的同时也造福社会。

Dedicating Your Love

Ancient characters of the Holy Bible, such as: Abraham, Job, King Saul, King David and others were said to be wealthy men of God in the scriptures①. It is said that these men obtained great wealth by giving 10% of their money away to God. God tells Abraham in the Old Testament to give Him 10% of all that he owns and he will be blessed financially because of it.

Great men and women of the 20th and in the 21st century say that giving money away actually makes themselves feel good and brings many blessings into their life. Businessmen such as Donald Trump, Warren Buffet and Bill Gates have all given money away and in return they have helped many people and they have been financially blessed②. Powerful and influential women such as Oprah Winfrey, Angelina Jolie and Martha Stewart are all said to be big donors and rich women. These women know how to draw wealth to themselves and plenty of it.

As you can see, we have a diverse group of people here. We have

---

① scripture [ˈskriptʃə] *n.* 经典,宗教的神圣作品

② blessed [ˈblesid] *adj.* 幸福的,快乐的

奉献爱心

古代圣经里的人物亚伯拉罕、约伯、索尔王、大卫王和其他人在经文中都被认为是上帝富有的孩子。据说，这些人因为把自己财产的10%分给上帝而获得了大量的财富。上帝在旧约里面告诉亚伯拉罕，把他全部财富的10%给予上帝，就会受到财富的保佑。

出生在20世纪、生活在21世纪的伟大的男士和女士们认为，捐出金钱确实使自己感觉良好，给他们的生活带来了很多祝福。唐纳德·特朗普、沃伦·巴菲特和比尔·盖茨等商业人士，已经捐出了金钱，作为回报，他们在帮助很多人的同时也获得了财富的保佑。据说，奥普拉·温弗瑞、安吉莉娜·朱丽和玛莎·斯图尔特等强势和有影响力的女性，都是大慈善家和富有的女人。这些女性知道如何敛财，有大把的财富。

正如你所看到的，在这里我们有不同的人群。我们有富裕的男人和女人。最为重要的是，他们来自不同的群体，有着不同的宗教背景。他们所有人看起来都很有钱。他们在各自的领域都是顶级

rich men and women. Most of all, they come from diverse groups and religious backgrounds. All of them seem to have money. They are known to be top experts in their areas. The interesting thing is that they are not all from the same religious background and they are all not preachers① or known for their great religious sermons②. How does a person get rich then? Is giving away your money and financial resources, truly a way to get rich? Did our parents teach us wrong when they told us to, "always hold onto our money for a rainy day?" The wealthiest people in the world are actually givers. They donate a lot of their money to charity and their time as well. In return, they seem to gain great wealth. Is there some type of financial energy that is becoming more obvious?

According to the movie, "The Secret", the best way to get anything is to ask for it. The movie teaches that the laws of attraction are indeed real and they work if you put them into practice. This is said to work for atheists, agnostics and believers in a particular religion. Is this really the secret to wealth?

It is amazing that most billionaires and millionaires come from different religious backgrounds. There are rich people in literally every faith around the world. However, many faiths teach that giving a portion of their money away actually helps people and brings wealth to you. If everyone is practicing a different faith and believing in something entirely different from someone else and still gaining wealth, then it means that

---

① preacher [ˈpriːtʃə] *n.* 说教者，鼓吹者

② sermon [ˈsəːmən] *n.* 布道，讲道

专家。有趣的是，他们来自不同的宗教背景，都不是布道者或因他们伟大的宗教布道而出名。那么一个人是怎样富起来的呢？把你的金钱和金融资源捐出去真是一种变富的方法吗？当父母教给我们“永远留钱以防万一”时，他们错了吗？世界上最富有的人其实是慈善家。他们把自己大量的钱捐给慈善事业和他们的时代。作为回报，他们似乎获得了很多财富。有变得更加明显的某种类型的金融能量吗？

根据电影《奥秘》的原则，得到东西最好的办法是展开追求。这部影片告诉我们，吸引法则确实存在，如果你把它们付诸实践，它们就起作用。据说这种法则对无神论者、不可知论者和特定宗教的信徒都起作用。这真的是通向富有的秘诀吗？

令人吃惊的是，大多数亿万富翁和百万富翁来自不同的宗教背景。世界上几乎每一种信仰确切地说都有富有的人。然而，很多信仰都教导我们捐出一部分金钱，实实在在地帮助别人的同时也会给你带来财富。如果每个人都持有不同的信仰，与其他人的信仰完全不同，仍然能够获得财富，那么，这就意味着吸引法则能够真正适用于任何渴望金钱或物质财富的人。

沙特阿拉伯据说是世界上最富裕的国家之一。这是一个把伊斯兰教作为主要宗教信仰的国家。据说，许多沙特人是亿万富翁，拥有庞大的财富。许多宗教都教导说，上帝祝福他自己的人民。然

the law of attraction can truly apply to anyone that desires money or material possessions.

Saudi Arabia is said to be one of the richest countries in the world. As we know, this is a country that considers the Muslim faith to be their primary religion. It is said that many Saudi's are billionaires and have tremendous wealth. Many religions teach that God blesses his own people. However, everyone that is on the Forbes.com richest persons list comes from different backgrounds from around the world. It is obvious that it does not make a difference what religious background you come from. What matters is that you are practicing the law of attraction.

Money does not seem to be given to us when we volunteer our time to do something. Instead, something nice may be done for you by someone else. Mother Theresa was one of the most giving women to ever have lived in the world. She volunteered a great portion of her life to the hurting and wounded children of Calcutta India. However she did not become a billionaire or a millionaire because of it. She died penniless and broke and with great admiration from the world that knew of her. Her energy brought happiness to the lives of thousands of people that needed her. However, she did not get rich.

Wealth is obtained by first asking for what you want from the spirit world. You must ask for it and believe that you will get it. You do not have to be educated to obtain wealth either. There are thousands of successful entrepreneurs who do not have any education beyond high school. Does having a college degree mean that you will instantly gain wealth of any sort? The answer to this question is no.

而，福布斯最富有的人员名单里，每一个人都来自世界不同的地方，不同的背景。很明显，你来自什么宗教背景并不重要，重要的是你正在实践吸引法则。

当我们自愿奉献我们的时间做一些有益的事时，我们似乎并没有得到什么钱。相反，有些好事可能有其他人已经为你做了。特雷莎修女是世界上最具奉献精神的女性之一，她把自己的大部分生命献给了印度加尔各答那些受伤害的孩子。然而，她却并没有因此而成为亿万富翁或百万富翁。她去世时身无分文，但却得到了全世界认识她的人的无限敬佩。她的精神给成千上万需要她的人带去了幸福，然而，她并没有变得富有。

获得财富首先要扪心自问，你想从精神世界中得到什么。你必须问这个问题，相信你能够得到它。为了获得财富你也不需要接受教育，成千上万的成功企业家也没有接受高中以外的教育。拥有大学学位就意味着你将立即获得某种财富吗？这个问题的答案是否定的。

很多人努力地创办自己的企业，以获得经济上的自由。但是，如果你看看财务方面成功的股票经纪人，你会发现，他们在为别人工作的同时收入仍高达数百万美元。同样，你也可以发现很多成功的房地产经纪人。很多房地产经纪人尽管已经很富裕，但仍在继续为成功的企业服务。他们可以很容易地用自己的名字开房地产公

Many people strive to start their own business to receive financial freedom. However, if you look at a financially successful stock broker, you will find that they are working for someone else and still earning millions of dollars. You can find the same with many successful real estate agents. Many real estate agents continue to work for successful companies despite becoming rich. They could easily start their own real estate office with their own name on it. However they choose to work for a real estate agency.

The power of gaining wealth seems to be given to those that want it and who are willing to give a portion of their wealth away to charities and others that are in need. Most wealthy people do not just give \$ 10.00 away, but they are literally giving away thousands, millions and even billions. They don't have to do this, but they are choosing to do this because they want to be able to help others that are in need. The rich usually get wealthy because they loved to work and they often worked long and hard hours. They mastered their craft and gave their money away at the same time. Slowly, they began to build their financial empires. We have found that most financially well off people tend to have a love for giving to others.

(984 words)

司，但他们却选择为地产中介机构工作。

获得财富的权力似乎是给予了这样的人，他们想要获得财富、愿意将部分财富捐给慈善机构和需要财富的其他人。大多数富人不是只捐10美元，他们实际上捐出了几千、百万甚至是上亿的钱。他们没有必要这样做，但是他们选择这样做，因为他们希望能够帮助那些需要帮助的人。富人通常得到财富是因为他们热爱工作，经常长时间、努力地工作。他们拥有自己的技能，同时也捐出了金钱。慢慢地，他们开始构建自己的金融帝国。我们会发现，大多数经济上富裕的人都具有为他人奉献的爱心。

知识链接

Giving 10% of their money away to God 什一税。欧洲基督教会向居民征收的一种宗教捐税，源起于《旧约》时代。根据这种制度，信徒要按照教会当局的规定或法律的要求，捐纳本人收入的十分之一供宗教事业之用，主要用于神职人员薪俸、教堂日常经费以及赈济。

题　记

人类有史以来就在为如何计算和测量幸福和快乐进行着不懈的探索。历史上许多伟大的哲学家、文学家对追求人生的幸福和快乐都留下了富有哲理的寓言、美丽的神话、动人的故事和脍炙人口的描述。而谢菲尔德大学的研究员季米特里·拉斯也正在编制英国的幸福地图，描绘国家财富的分布与人们的幸福感之间的关系。结果显示，随着贫富差距的增大，快乐的人和痛苦的人之间的鸿沟也随之增大。友谊可能是快乐和幸福的最大源泉之一，但是结交朋友和维持友情的能力却明显受到金钱的影响。金钱是获得社交、尊严和尊重的门票。欧洲人的研究再次陷入了郁闷的怪圈：追求幸福和快乐的愿望是美好的，可悲的是，在物欲横流的今天，通往地狱的道路恰恰是由这种美好的愿望铺成的。

The Source of Enjoyment

Money may not be able to buy you love, but what about happiness? Sarah Freeman reports on new research hoping to pinpoint the most contented place in Britain.

There have recently been a host of cautionary① tales about the uneasy relationship between wealth and happiness. On his 33rd birthday, Robbie Williams, a man who has made millions from his music career, checked into an Arizona clinic where he spent three weeks being treated for a dependency on prescription drugs. The singer was widely acknowledged to have emerged triumphant from the Take That split, but, as he continued with an "after-care program" in Los Angeles, his former bandmates were celebrating a Brit Award, another number one single and the prospect of a UK tour. While Robbie has been keeping a low profile, Britney Spears has become a walking advert for the perils② of fame and fortune. In the last few weeks, the shaven-headed singer has been in and

---

① cautionary [ˈkɔːʃənəri] *a.* 警戒的

② peril [ˈperil] *n.* 危机,危险的事物

快乐的源泉

金钱可能无法买到爱，但是能买到幸福么？ 莎拉·弗里曼报告了一项新的研究，希望精确地描述英国最具幸福感的地区。

最近发生了许多有借鉴意义的事情，表明财富和幸福之间的关系并不和谐。 罗比·威廉斯，一位在音乐事业上已经赚了数百万的男士，在33岁生日当天，被送进亚利桑那州的一家诊所，在那里接受了三周的治疗，因为他对医生给他开的处方药有依赖性。 这位歌手从“接招”组合分离出来之后，引起了广泛的瞩目，取得了骄人的成绩。 就在他继续留在洛杉矶接受“病后护理和治疗”的时候，他的前队友正在庆祝一个“全英音乐奖”，推出又一张排名第一的单曲和前景美好的英国巡演。 尽管罗比一直保持低调，布兰妮·斯皮尔斯却正在为名利冒险，四处做广告。 在过去的几个星期，当这位光头歌手进出戒毒所之时，布兰妮正在极力应付她的巨额财富也无法缓解的问题。

然而，尽管健康的银行资产、股票和证券投资组合以及大量的

out of rehab as she struggles to deal with problems from which her vast fortune can offer little relief.

However, while a healthy bank balance, a portfolio of stocks and shares and a fistful of Premium Bonds, may not be able to buy peace of mind and, ultimately, happiness, there is, it seems, a link between finances and the feel good factor. "Obviously individual happiness is very much dependent on life events," says University of Sheffield researcher Dimitris Ballas, who is compiling a happiness map of Britain. "At one end you have things such as starting a new relationship and winning promotion at work, and at the other, you have bereavement① and poor health. Often these are things which we don't have control over, but part of what we have been looking at is how the distribution of wealth across the country is linked to how happy people feel."

Once complete, the research, part of the Understanding Population Trends and Process project, which is being co-ordinated by the University of Leeds, will reveal not just which is the happiest town and city in England, but pinpoint exactly which areas in those towns and cities have the most contended② residents. The map will be based on information gathered from the British Household Panel Survey, but, as the gap between rich and poor has widened, it already seems the chasm③ between

① bereavement [bi'riːvmənt] *n.*(亲人)丧亡

② contend [kən'tend] *v.* 主张,争辩

③ chasm [kæzəm] *n.* 大差别,代沟

优质债券不可能买来心灵的安宁和最终的幸福，但是看上去，财富和良好感觉之间还是存在某种联系。谢菲尔德大学的研究员季米特里·拉斯正在编制英国的幸福地图，他认为，“很明显，个人的幸福在很大程度上取决于生活中的事件。一方面，你要关注新的人际交往、工作晋升等问题；另一方面，你又要面临丧亲之痛和健康状况下降这些无法控制的事件。然而，我们已经观察到的部分问题是，国家财富的分布与人们的幸福感有关”。

“理解人口的发展趋势和过程”项目的部分研究一旦完成，不仅将揭示英国最快乐的市镇和城市，而且还将精确描述这些市镇和城市的哪些地区生活着最具有满足感的居民。利兹大学是这项研究的合作者。这张地图依据的信息来自“英国家庭专门调查”，但是，随着贫富差距的增大，快乐的人和痛苦的人之间的鸿沟也随之增大。

季米特里指出：“财富的分布对幸福程度产生了巨大影响。”20世纪的前50年，贫富差距在最重要的领域开始缩小。例如，婴儿死亡率和受教育的机会都得到了很大的改善。早在20世纪50年代，研究表明，与前半个世纪相比，贫困几乎已经被社会改革消除。当然并没有完全消除，但我们也很容易忘记那些年取得的成果，我们经历了多么艰苦的奋斗。然而，这种状态并没有按照那种方式持续太久。虽然平均工资得到了明显的

the pleased and the miserable has grown.

"The distribution of wealth can have a huge impact on levels of happiness," says Dimitris. In the first 50 years of the last century the gaps between the rich and the poor narrowed in what were the most important areas. The chances of children dying as infants, for example, and the opportunities in education improved and, in the early 1950s, research suggested that compared to half a century earlier, poverty had all but been eliminated by social reform. It hadn't of course, but it's easy to forget just what had been achieved in those years and how hard it was fought for. However, the status quo such as it was didn't stay that way for long. Although average salaries have grown significantly, at the bottom of the scale, there has been little or no rise in real income. Add to that the fact that the areas which suffered the least in the recession of the early 1980s tended to gain most in the subsequent recovery, and the most depressed areas struggled to recover ground; in terms of distribution of wealth, Britain has become polarized.

Initial findings show that in Yorkshire, York, the city with the highest percentage of adults with degrees and the lowest amount claiming job seekers allowance and income support in the county tops the happiness scale, followed by Leeds, Sheffield, Bradford and finally Hull.

More detailed analysis is now underway and, with the likes of David Cameron arguing that improving people's happiness is a key challenge for politicians, and calling for a shift in emphasis from GDP to what he called GWB (general well-being) it could well become a blueprint for

提高，但对于社会底层的人来说，实际收入的提高微乎其微，或者说根本没有增加。此外，还存在着这样一个事实，20世纪80年代早期受经济衰退影响最小的地区在随后的恢复期财富增长最快，受经济萧条影响最严重的地区却在艰难地恢复发展。根据财富的分布，英国已经两极分化。

初步调查发现，约克地区的约克郡，这座有着最多高学历成人、最少要求求职者津贴和收入支持比率的城市，竟然占据幸福排行榜的榜首，随后是利兹、唐卡斯特、布拉德福德以及排在最后的赫尔。

进一步的详细分析正在进行中，正如大卫·卡梅伦所说，改善人民的生活是政治家面临的核心挑战，并呼吁把关注的重点从国内生产总值转移到国民幸福指数(general well-being)，这可以适当列入国家政策和社会改革的计划。季米特里认为，“这可能是一个简略的概括”。例如，2005年时，在整个英格兰和威尔士地区，收入最低的是伯明翰市的斯帕克布洛和小希思。当年有两个晚上还发生了现场大骚乱。当然，这种骚乱爆发的原因极其复杂，但是收入远不只是一种购物的手段，它也可被看做是一种指标，用来衡量我们自身具有什么样的价值，而某些衡量指标又如何评估它们自己的价值。金钱本身不能吃，不能提供温暖，是可怜的伙伴，但是，在维持生计之外，它买来了闲暇时间和活动的权利。

public policy and social change. "It may be a crude summary," says Dimitris. But for example, in 2005, across all of England and Wales, incomes were at their lowest in Birmingham's Sparkbrook and Small Heath constituency. In the same year over two nights it was also the scene of major riots. Obviously the reasons behind an outbreak of violence like that are incredibly complex, but income is much more than a means to buy things. It can also be seen as an indicator of how we are valued and for some a measure of how they value themselves. Money itself cannot be eaten, provides no warmth and makes poor company, but, above subsistence level, it buys the right to leisure time and activities. Friendship may be one of the biggest sources of happiness and well-being, but the ability to make and maintain friends is significantly affected by income. Money is a ticket to social interaction, to dignity and respect, and understanding how the distribution of wealth affects the well-being of a nation is vitally important for those responsible for social policy.

(853 words)

友谊可能是快乐和幸福的最大源泉之一，但是结交朋友和维持友情的能力却明显受到收入的影响。金钱是获得社交、尊严和尊重的门票。理解财富的分配对国家福祉的影响对那些负责社会政策的人极其重要。

知识链接

Take That “接招”组合是20世纪80年代至90年代前半段英国最走红的青春流行乐队，当时几乎主宰了整个英国排行榜。这支被称为“英国的新街边仔”乐队的音乐与“披头士”一样，由节奏与布鲁斯·城市灵歌和主流流行音乐元素组成，但更舞曲化、成人化。其俊美性感的外形赢得了大量少男少女崇拜者，而其感性优美的音乐旋律同样可以打动成人听众的心弦。在不列颠流行乐的冲击下，“接招”于1996年解散，“绿洲”组合全面取代了他们的地位。但这支制造了英国青春流行音乐热潮现象的乐队理应被载入摇滚乐的史册。

Brit Award 全英音乐奖(或简称The BRITs)是由英国唱片业协会(BPI)创办的、一年一度的流行音乐奖。

题　记

根据美国TNS金融服务公司近日公布的一项年度市场报告，美国国内净资产超过100万美元的富翁人数创出新高，达到890万。在这个盛产百万富翁的国度，“自制百万富翁的秘密”正在给渴望财富的人们酿造一盘饕餮大餐。心理学大师荣格说过：“任何下意识的欲望与振(震)动，都会成真。”杰夫·哈里斯能够踏上通往财富之路源自于强大的自信，永远相信自己可以在财务方面成就一番事业。史蒂夫·麦克斯韦尔通过自我教育学会了投资，即消费不能超过收入，而积攒下来的钱要用于投资能增值的项目。吉尔·斯特拉恩之所以能成为北美地区前25名女性商业领袖之一，要归功于她积极的工作态度、充满梦想的生活热情和持之以恒的心灵意志。世界上没有不可能，要达到成功，就要像百万富翁那样——学会驾驭自己的心智。

Secrets of Self-Made Millionaires

When you think "millionaire," what image comes to mind? For many of us, it's a flashy Wall Street banker type who flies a private jet, collects cars and lives the kind of decadent lifestyle that would make Donald Trump proud. But many modern millionaires live in middle-class neighborhoods, work full-time and shop in discount stores like the rest of us. What motivates them isn't material possessions but the choices that money can bring. "For the rich, it's not about getting more stuff. It's about having the freedom to make almost any decision you want," says T. Harv Eker, author of Secrets of the Millionaire Mind. Wealth means you can send your child to any school or quit a job you don't like. Here, several people who have at least a million dollars in liquid assets share the secrets that helped them get there.

Twenty years ago, Jeff Harris hardly seemed on the road to wealth. He was a college dropout who struggled to support his wife, DeAnn, and three kids, working as a grocery store clerk and at a junkyard① where he melted scrap metal alongside convicts. "At times we were so broke that

① junkyard[ˈdʒʌŋkjɑːd] *n.* 废旧物堆积的地方

自制百万富翁的秘密

当你想到“百万富翁”时，脑海里会出现什么样的形象呢？对我们许多人来说，那是一个庸俗而华丽的华尔街银行家的形象，拥有私人飞机，豪车云集，生活腐朽颓废，而这一切却令唐纳德·特朗普感到自豪。但是，许多现代的百万富翁却住在中产阶级社区，全天工作，和我们其他人一样在折扣商店买东西。他们成功的动力不是物质财富，而是金钱可以带来的选择。《百万富翁的秘密》一书的作者哈维·艾克说：“对于富人来说，这并不是要获得更多的东西。而是拥有做任何想做的决定的自由。”财富意味着可以将你的孩子送去任何学校读书，或者辞去你不喜欢的工作。几位至少拥有100万美元流动资产的人士在此分享了他们成功的秘密。

二十年前，根本看不出杰夫·哈里斯能踏上通往财富之路。当时他从大学辍学，靠在杂货店做职员以及在垃圾场和罪犯们一起熔炼金属碎片，艰难地维持妻子蒂安和三个孩子的生活。“有时，我们穷得连上自助洗衣店的钱都没有，只得在浴缸里洗衣服。”现在，他已经是南卡罗莱纳州约克县的一位49岁的投资顾问和拥有数百万美元家财的富豪。杰夫脱贫致富的一个主要原因是：他始终认为自己

we washed our clothes in the bathtub because we couldn't afford the Laundromat." Now he's a 49-year-old investment advisor and multimillionaire in York, South Carolina. There was one big reason Jeff pulled ahead of the pack: He always knew he'd be rich. The reality is that 80 percent of Americans worth at least $5 million grew up in middle-class or lesser households, just like Jeff. Wanting to be wealthy is a crucial first step. Says Eker, "The biggest obstacle to wealth is fear. People are afraid to think big, but if you think small, you'll only achieve small things." It all started for Jeff when he met a stockbroker at a Christmas party. "Talking to him, it felt like discovering fire," he says. "I started reading books about investing during my breaks at the grocery store, and I began putting $25 a month in a mutual fund." Next he taught a class at a local community college on investing. His students became his first clients, which led to his investment practice. "There were lots of struggles," says Jeff, "but what got me through it was believing with all my heart that I would succeed."

When Steve Maxwell graduated from college, he had an engineering degree and a high-tech job — but he couldn't balance his checkbook. "I took one finance class in college but dropped it to go on a ski trip," says the 45-year-old father of three, who lives in Windsor, Colorado. "I actually had to go to my bank and ask them to teach me how to read my statement." One of the biggest obstacles to making money is not understanding it: Thousands of us avoid investing because we just don't get it. But to make money, you must be financially literate. "It bothered me that I didn't understand this stuff," says Steve, "so I read books and

会富有。现实情况是，就像杰夫一样，80%至少拥有500万美元的美国人都来自中产阶级或较差一点的家庭。想要成为富人是至关重要的第一步。艾克认为，“最大的障碍是对财富的恐惧。人们害怕想象巨大的成功，但如果你只想获得小的成功，那就只能安于现状”。杰夫的成功始于一次圣诞晚会，他在那里遇见了一位股票经纪人。他说：“与他交谈，感觉就像发现了思想的火花。我开始在杂货店里休息时阅读有关投资的书，开始每个月花25美元投资共同基金。”接着，他在当地社区学院教授投资课程。他的学生成为他的第一批客户，从此步入投资行业。杰夫声称：“有很多困难。但让我克服困难的动力是我全身心地相信，我一定会成功。”

史蒂夫·麦克斯韦尔大学毕业时，获得了工程学位，也找到了一份高科技的工作，但他的收支仍然难以保持平衡。这位45岁、三个孩子的父亲，住在科罗拉多州的温莎市。他说：“我在大学修了一门金融类的课程，但还是逃课滑雪去了。我真的不得不去银行，并要求他们教我阅读账单。”赚钱的最大障碍之一是不懂钱：成千上万的人避免投资就是因为不了解投资。但为了赚钱，你必须掌握一定的财务知识。史蒂夫说：“但困扰我的是我根本不明白这些东西。于是，我就阅读与资金管理和投资相关的书籍和杂志，我请教我认识的每一位金融怪杰，让他们解释给我听。”

他和妻子开始学以致用：想办法克服入不敷出的状况。他们不再盲目地买东西，无论是买车、付有线电视账单，还是购置家具，总会协商以达成更好的交易，在有能力购买更贵的东西之前，这些

magazines about money management and investing, and I asked every financial whiz① I knew to explain things to me."

He and his wife started applying the lessons: They made a point to live below their means. They never bought on impulse, always negotiated better deals on their cars, cable bills, furniture, and stayed in their home long after they could afford a more expensive one. They also put 20 percent of their annual salary into investments. Within ten years, they were millionaires, and people were coming to Steve for advice. "Someone would say, 'I need to refinance my house — what should I do?' A lot of times, I wouldn't know the answer, but I'd go find it and learn something in the process," he says.

In 2003, Steve quit his job to become part owner of a company that holds personal finance seminars for employees of corporations like Wal-Mart. He also started going to real estate investment seminars, and it's paid off: He now owns $30 million worth of investment properties, including apartment complexes, a shopping mall and a quarry. "I was an engineer who never thought this life was possible, but all it truly takes is a little self-education," says Steve. "You can do anything once you understand the basics."

In 1995, Jill Blashack Strahan and her husband were barely making ends meet. Like so many of us, Jill was eager to discover her purpose, so she splurged② on a session with a life coach. "When I told her my goal

---

① whiz[hwiz] *n.* 怪才
② splurge[splə:dʒ] *vt.* & *vi.* 乱花(钱),挥霍

物品会留在家中用很长一段时间。他们还将年薪的20%拿出来做投资。10年内，他们成为了百万富翁。人们来找史蒂夫咨询，他说："有人问：'我需要对我的房子再投资，该怎么办?'很多时候，我也不知道答案，但我会去寻找，并在寻找的过程中了解情况。"

2003年，史蒂夫辞去工作，成为一家公司的合伙人，这家公司为像沃尔玛这样的公司员工举办个人财务研讨会。他也开始参加房地产投资研讨会，并获得了回报：他现在拥有价值3 000万美元的投资物业，包括公寓楼、一家购物中心和一个石矿。史蒂夫说："我是一名工程师，从未想过可以过上这样的生活，但这需要的付出仅仅是一点自我教育而已。一旦你理解了基本法则，就可以做任何事情。"

1995年，吉尔·斯特拉恩与丈夫几乎入不敷出。像我们许多人一样，吉尔渴望发现她的价值，于是，她花了一大笔钱跟一位生活教练上培训课。"当我告诉她，我的目标是一年挣3万美元时，她说我设定的标准太低。我需要把我的重点放在激情而不是薪水上。"吉尔和儿子生活在明尼苏达州的亚历山大市，拥有一个礼品篮公司，一年只赚1.5万美元。她注意到，当她让潜在的客户品尝食品时，篮子的销量就会疯长。吉尔就想，为什么不直接将食物放在一个有趣的包装里卖给顾客呢?

拿着6千美元的存款、一份银行贷款和一个朋友的投资，吉尔开始在后院的小棚子里包装美食，然后试尝在派对上卖给顾客。这也不是件易事。"我记得有一天坐在外面，想着我已经有三个月没交

was to make $ 30,000 a year, she said I was setting the bar too low. I needed to focus on my passion, not on the paycheck." Jill, who lives with her son in Alexandria, Minnesota, owned a gift basket company and earned just $ 15,000 a year. She noticed when she let potential buyers taste the food items, the baskets sold like crazy. Jill thought, Why not sell the food directly to customers in a fun setting?

With $ 6,000 in savings, a bank loan and a friend's investment, Jill started packaging gourmet foods in a backyard shed and selling them at taste-testing parties. It wasn't easy. "I remember sitting outside one day, thinking we were three months behind on our house payment, I had two employees I couldn't pay, and I ought to get a real job. But then I thought, No, this is your dream. Recommit and get to work." She stuck with it, even after her husband died three years later. "I live by the law of abundance, meaning that even when there are challenges in life, I look for the win-win," she says. The positive attitude worked: Jill's backyard company, Tastefully Simple, is now a direct-sales business, with $ 120 million in sales last year. And Jill was named one of the top 25 female business owners in North America by Fast Company magazine.

According to research by Thomas J. Stanley, author of The Millionaire Mind, over 80 percent of millionaires say they never would have been successful if their vocation wasn't something they cared about.

(1,015 words)

房租了，还有两个员工的工资也没有支付，我必须得找一份真正的工作。 但是转念一想，不，这就是你的梦想。 于是再次下定决心开始工作。”她一直坚持着，甚至在丈夫三年后去世了也没放弃。她说：“我满怀热情地生活，即使生活中充满挑战，我也期待着双赢。”她积极的工作态度起了作用：吉尔家的后院公司——“品味简单“，现在已成为一家直销公司，去年的销售额达 1.2 亿美元。 吉尔被《快速公司》杂志评为北美地区前 25 名女性商业领袖之一。

根据《百万富翁的秘密》一书的作者托马斯·斯坦利的研究，80% 以上的百万富翁认为，如果他们的职业不是自己所关心的，他们永远不会取得成功。

知识链接

Fast Company 《快速公司》杂志是与《财富》和《商业周刊》齐名的美国最具影响力的商业杂志之一。1995 年由两位前《哈佛商业评论》编辑艾伦·韦伯和比尔·泰勒创刊，秉承“世界的变革正在改变商业，商业正在改变世界”的理念，为欲创造财富和变革商业的人士提供有关规模管理、主导议题和技术的最新思想。《快速公司》杂志每年会在全球范围内寻找具有创造性商业理念、增长速度快、具备一定社会公益性的企业(或个人)，通过资深的专业记者的投票，评选出 50 名年度企业或个人，称为“Fast 50”。

题 记

感受幸福是件很困难的事，那是一种灯火阑珊处的境界；专注幸福是一种感恩，那是经历岁月流年后的生活态度。但是，我们的思维一直飘忽不定：开车时，脑海中会浮现出与配偶的争斗；早上刷牙时，大脑会重现与朋友的狂野派对。当人们对身边的事漠不关心时，幸福感就会下降。而思维一旦游移快乐的记忆，幸福对我们来说就会遥不可及。浪漫的巴黎蜜月使人想起索价过高的旅馆中流鼻涕的侍者；穿越繁忙的交通来不及观看城市中高楼叠嶂的风景就如流水卷动河沙一般停滞在红绿灯下。专注幸福让我们从梦中惊醒：每天专心做事、训练专注力、专心致志读一本好书或看一场电影、尽量不要同时做多件事、每天冥想 5 至 10 分钟。专注幸福的方式简单而又朴实，却能够将幸福留在我们身边。

Keeping Your Focus on Happiness

Nearly half the time we're awake, our thoughts drift to topics unrelated to whatever we're doing. We think about the fight we had with our spouse when we're driving or replay events from a friend's wild party while brushing our teeth in the morning. We text incessantly while watching TV and phone mom during laundry-folding time. And all the while our minds are wandering — even when we're having pleasant daydreams — we're not very happy, according to a new study published in the journal Science. "How often peoples, minds wander is definitely a big predictor of who's happy and who's not happy," says study author Matthew Killingsworth, a doctoral candidate in psychology at Harvard University, because the more often they take themselves out of the present moment, the less happy they are.

The study found that happiness falls when folks aren't focused on the task at hand, even an unenjoyable one, like doing errands①. The researchers used a novel approach to get real-time snapshots of what the 2,250 study participants were thinking and how they felt throughout the day. They developed a free iPhone app that buzzed volunteers, whose

① errand [ˈerənd] *n.* 差事

保持对幸福的专注

我们有近一半的时间是清醒的，我们的思维漂移到与我们所做的毫不相关的主题上。我们开车时，脑海中会浮现出与配偶的争斗；早上刷牙时，大脑会重现与朋友的狂野派对。我们一边不断发短信一边看电视，在整理洗好的衣服时给妈妈打电话。根据《科学》杂志发表的一项最新研究，我们的思维一直飘忽不定，即使我们拥有愉快的白日梦——我们都很不高兴。哈佛大学心理学在读博士生、本项研究的作者马修·基林斯沃思认为，“思维漫游的频率，绝对是人们快乐与否的主要预测范式”。因为他们越频繁地脱离现实，他们的快乐就越少。

研究发现，当人们不怎么关注身边的任务——即使是出差这种无趣的事时，幸福感就会下降。研究人员采用了一种新方法，对2 250名研究参与者实时拍照，考察他们正在想什么，以及他们在一天中的感受。他们开发了一种免费的 iPhone 苹果应用程序，让这些平均年龄为 34 岁的志愿者用这种蜂鸣器向外发出信号，并每日数次询问他们在接触这些应用程序之前心情如何，他们正在做什么，以及他们是否正在思考其他的事情，而不是他们正在做的事情。除了

average age was 34, several times a day asking them how they were feeling right before they were contacted, what they were doing and whether they were thinking about something other than what they were doing. Except during sex, participants recorded their minds wandering during every activity; most frequently, minds drifted off during personal grooming① like taking a shower, shaving, and putting on makeup.

Most of the daydreams were about unpleasant or neutral topics, like mental to-do lists. But even pleasurable mental fantasies left participants no happier than when they were focused on whatever activity they were doing: weaving through traffic, tying their shoes, writing out a check. How the heck can this be? "When the mind wanders to a happy memory, it tends to eventually turn back to things that aren't quite as positive," says health psychologist Kelly McGonigal, who teaches a class on the science of willpower at Stanford University. Reminiscing about, say, that romantic Paris honeymoon might land you thinking about the snotty② bellhop at the overpriced hotel where you stayed. This is the brain returning to what brain researchers refer to as its "default mode," a state of contemplating the past to learn from it, the future to prepare for it, or things in the present to see what needs to be fixed, explains Killingsworth. This default mode probably gave us an evolutionary advantage by making us alert to dangers while we were hunting and gathering. "We maximized our survival chances even if we didn't maximize our happiness," says McGonigal. "Evolution doesn't give a

① grooming *n.* 修饰

② snotty [ˈsnɔti] *adj.* 下贱的

性生活，参与者记录了每一种活动期间的思维飘忽状态。思维在洗澡、刮胡子和化妆之类的个人修饰期间游离得最频繁。

大多数的白日梦是关于不愉快或中性的话题，如思绪混乱地列出要做的事情。但即使是愉快的心理幻想也不如参与者关注自己正在做的活动更快乐，如穿越繁忙的交通，系鞋带和开支票。怎么会是这样呢？健康心理学家凯利·麦戈尼盖尔在斯坦福大学教授意志力科学课程，她认为，“当思维游移到快乐的记忆，它往往最终又回到并不那么乐观的事情上”。回忆一下，例如，浪漫的巴黎蜜月可能使你想起曾经待过的索价过高的旅馆中流鼻涕的侍者。基林斯沃思解释说，这是大脑回到大脑研究人员所指的“默认模式”，即一种状态，思考过去以吸取教训；思考未来以做好准备；或者思考现在，看有哪些需要解决的问题。这种默认模式可能给了我们一种进化优势，当我们在打猎和采集时，保持对危险的警觉。麦戈尼盖尔认为，“即使我们没有让幸福最大化，也要让生存机会最大化。进化毫不在乎幸福”。

但我们目前并不关心剑齿虎，我们的确在乎我们的幸福。我们可以做些什么以防止思维不断逃离现实呢？麦戈尼盖尔认为，如果我们像肌肉训练那样定期练习一些特定的技能，就能够集中精力或注意力。可以尝试以下方法：

每天专心做事。做事时不要让思维游移。研究表明，早上练习少许注意力的人更有能力保持全天的关注度。淋浴是个不错的选择，你可以独处，不受打扰。在整个沐浴过程中全神贯注，注

damn about happiness."

But these days we don't worry about saber-toothed tigers, and we do give a damn about our happiness. So what can we do to get keep our thoughts from continuously fleeing the present moment? McGonigal says our mental focus, or mindfulness, can be built up, like a muscle, if we practice certain skills regularly. Try the following:

Start the day with a focused task. And don't allow your mind to wander while you do it. Research suggests that those who practice a little mindfulness in the morning have a better ability to stay focused throughout the day. A good task to choose might be the shower, where you're alone and free of interruptions. Be fully present during your entire shower, and pay attention to sensory experience. Feel the water, smell the shampoo, notice what your hands feel like when they soap your skin. Take note of the glass fogging up and the sound of the water hitting the shower door or curtain.

Exercise with mindfulness. Any sort of activity you do — walking, running, biking, swimming — can help increase mental focus by boosting blood flow in the brain. But you can add mindfulness to your workouts by consciously shifting your attention to certain sensations while you exercise. Try this on your next walk or run: First feel your breath, and let the sound of your inhales and exhales register. Then focus on your feet hitting the earth. What sensations do you feel in your legs? Next shift your attention to any sounds you hear, then what you see. After that, focus on yourself in contact with your environment, the sun on your skin, the rain on your forehead. Spend about a minute on each sensation before shifting your focus to a new one.

重感官体验。感受清水和洗发水的味道，注意用手把肥皂抹在皮肤上的感受。注意玻璃蒙上的水汽和水滴在淋浴门或门帘上的声音。

训练专注力。你做的任何活动，如散步、跑步、骑自行车、游泳等，都可以通过加速大脑的血液流动增强注意力。但是，你可以有意识地改变锻炼时对某些感觉的关注，从而增加训练中的专注力。在下一次散步或跑步时尝试下列做法：首先感觉一下呼吸，记住吸气和呼气的声音，然后全身心地注意撞击地面的脚，你的腿上是什么感觉？再转而注意你听到的任何声音，而后才是你看到的。在此之后，专注自己接触的环境，照在皮肤上的阳光，落在额头的雨水。每种感觉大约花一分钟的时间去体验，然后再将注意力转向新的事物。

专心致志读一本好书或看一场电影。只要你不让自己被电话铃声或黑莓手机的嗡嗡声分心，读一本引人入胜的书或看一场特别有吸引力的电影或电视节目，是一种练习注意力的了不起的方式。

尽量不要同时做多件事。同时做多件事是注意力的敌人；和朋友共进午餐时停止发短信；帮孩子做家庭作业时不要查收电子邮件；接听客户电话时停止浏览网页。如果你仍然感到大脑在游离，就迫使注意力重新集中到手头的工作上。听到你正在听的声音，阅读面前报告上的文字，注视即将切入你车道的汽车。

每天练习 5 至 10 分钟的冥想。显然，我们大多数人对冥想不

Immerse yourself in a good book or movie. Reading a page-turner or watching a compelling movie or TV show can be a great way to practice mindfulness, provided that you don't allow yourself to be distracted by, say, a ringing phone or buzzing Blackberry.

Minimize multi-tasking. It's the enemy of mindfulness. Stop the texting while having lunch with friends. Don't check your E-mail when you're helping the kids with homework. And stop scanning the internet when you get a call from a client. If you still sense your mind wandering, force your attention back to the task at hand. Hear the voice you're listening to; read the words on the report in front of you; watch the car that's about to cut into your lane.

Practice five to 10 minutes of daily meditation①. Sure, most of us don't have a clue about meditating, but that's what the internet was invented for. McGonigal has a free audio meditation session you can listen to, and mindfulness expert Jon Kabat-Zinn has posted a free video of a meditation class he gave to Google executives. The benefits? Those who practice regular meditation snap out of the brain's default wandering mode much faster than those who don't, according to a study from Emory University School of Medicine. They are also practicing a little defensive medicine. If you meditate regularly, you'll prevent the cognitive decline in attention span that naturally occurs with aging.

(984 words)

① meditation [ˌmediˈteiʃən] *n.* 冥想

太了解，这就是为什么要发明互联网。你可以听麦戈尼盖尔发布的免费冥想音频，也可以看注意力专家乔恩·卡巴金博士发布的免费冥想视频，这是他给谷歌高管上的课程。好处是什么呢？根据埃默里大学医学院的研究，相比那些不练习冥想的人，那些经常有规律地练习冥想的人跳出大脑默认漫游模式的速度要快得多。他们也练习一点防御性医疗。如果你有规律地思索，就会阻止注意力持续出现认知能力下降的现象，注意力的认知能力衰退将随着年龄的增长而自然产生。

知识链接

Blackberry 黑莓手机是一种采用双向寻呼模式的移动邮件系统，兼容现有的无线数据链路。在“9·11”事件中，美国通信设备几乎全线瘫痪，但时任美国副总统切尼的手机有黑莓功能，成功地进行了无线互联，能够随时随地接收关于灾难现场的实时信息。之后，美国掀起了一阵黑莓热潮。黑莓手机不仅成为企业高管、咨询顾问和华尔街商人常备的便携式电子邮件设备，美国国会甚至给每位议员配备了一部黑莓手机处理国事。

题　记

在市场经济时代，财富是衡量一个人成功与否的重要社会标志。之所以你被认为是一名成功者，多半是因为你拥有比别人多的财富。就像人们经常谈论曾经的世界首富比尔·盖茨一样。财富作为最真实和量化的尺度，反映出一个人的经济成就和社会地位。但是当你问及人们，他们是否愿意成为仅仅拥有高净值财富的人时，大部分人都会说不。因为成功最终并不是取决于金钱和声望的简单答案，而是取决于从金钱和声望之中找到更加复杂的答案。从广义的角度来看，成功意味着不浪费时间、做你最擅长的事、热爱你的工作、感受工作和生活的联系。这种简单的生活平衡给人们带来了身心愉悦的快感和心灵的净化与升华。据说上帝也不知道什么叫成功，曾经化装来到人间，想问问普通人究竟什么叫做成功。

A Balanced Life

Researchers have tried for years to find out what people really want. As labor markets become tighter and tighter, the answer to the question, "What do you really want out of your life?" becomes more and more serious. The traditional answer — and the answer that more than 75 percent of people actually will give — is simple: Money. More money. A lot of money.

There are a couple of ways to think about this. One is in terms of happiness. Studies consistently have shown that if you give people more money — and nothing else changes — they are no happier after they have the money than before. Another way to think about it is in terms of what people are willing to do to get more money. You might think about this question yourself. What would you be willing to do to earn significantly more money? Would you move to a different city? Would you work most weekends? Would you travel every week? Would you give up vacations and free time? Would you give up your marriage? How about your relationship with your children? Where would you stop?

It may actually be that having more money is not the greatest good. It might be that, if you stopped and thought about it, you could define several factors in your life that are more important than more money. This is why we want to think about a new definition of success. When we think about successful people, we tend to think about various high-powered

平衡的生活

研究人员多年来一直试图发现人们到底想要什么。由于劳动力市场越来越紧缩，“你究竟想从生活中得到什么？”这个问题的答案变得越来越重要。传统的答案很简单：金钱。比较多的金钱，很多的金钱。这也是75%以上的人给出的实际答案。

理解这个现象有几种方式。一种是用幸福感来衡量。大量的研究一致表明，如果给人们更多的钱，而其他方面完全不变，他们在有钱之后并不比以前更幸福。另一种思考这个问题的方式是考察人们赚了更多的钱后想做什么。你可以自己思考一下这个问题。赚了更多的大钱后你想做什么？你想搬到另一个城市去吗？你想周末多上班吗？你想每周出差吗？你想放弃假期和休闲时间吗？你想放弃婚姻吗？你和孩子之间的关系怎么样呢？你想在哪儿停下来？

事实上，赚更多的钱不一定是最好的事。如果你停下来，好好想一想，就会发现，生活中有几个因素比赚更多的钱重要得多。这就是为什么我们要思考成功的新定义。当我们想到成功人士的时候，头脑中会浮现出各种各样精力充沛的经理主管人员和高调的职业人士，他们确实容易引起我们的注意。成功的首要标准显然是金

executives and high-profile professionals who have caught our attention. The first yardstick[①] of success obviously is money. But when you ask people if they want to be like these individuals who each have a high net worth, many will say no. The reason: They have no desire, really, to live lives as driven as they perceive these people are. So, what does success mean, if we are asking in a larger sense of the word?

Don't waste time. "The most precious commodity in the world to me is time," says Dan, a training consultant. "You just have a fixed amount of life to live, and then you're finished. I don't want to waste a single second of mine. Success, to me, is being able to spend my time doing things that are meaningful and fun to me, and not spending a lot of my time doing things that are boring or meaningless."

Do what you do best. "When I get up in the morning, I feel absolutely clear that I can focus almost all of my day on work that I am sublimely[②] good at," says Carl, a bank executive. "To me, success is being able to know what my talents are and being able to use those talents every day, all day. I go home at night and feel that I've really made a contribution to the bank, and that the bank is making a contribution to society. I feel proud of my role there, and proud of the fact that I can do what I do really well."

Love what you do. "I just love feeling excited in the morning about making a contribution," says Tom, a well-known writer on the environment and conservation. "I can't think of anything I would do if I didn't feel passionate[③] about it. Otherwise, why do it? I'vebeen interested in the outdoors since I was a child in Alabama. I have followed that

---

① yardstick [ˈjɑːdstik] *n.* 比较标准

② sublime[səˈblaim] *adj.* 崇高的,庄严的

③ passionate[ˈpæʃənət] *adj.* 易动情的,多情的

钱。但是当你问及人们，他们是否愿意成为仅仅拥有高净值财富的人时，大部分人都会说不。其原因是他们真的不想过那种不得已的生活，就像他们看到的那些人一样。那么，从广义的角度来看，成功究竟意味着什么?

不浪费时间。培训顾问丹说："对我来说，世界上最珍贵的商品是时间。你活在世上的生命是有限的，之后你就将不复存在。每一秒钟我都不想浪费。对我来说，成功就是把时间花在对自己有意义和有趣的事上，而不是在无聊或无意义的事上浪费太多的时间。"

做你最擅长的事。银行行政人员卡尔说："当我早上起来的时候，我感觉非常清醒，我这一天要集中几乎所有的精力做我最擅长的事。对我而言，成功是能了解我的能力是什么，每天能够运用这些能力。晚上我回到家时，感觉到我对银行确实做出了贡献，而银行也对社会做出了贡献。我为我在银行所扮演的角色感到自豪，对我能够把我最擅长的事情做好而感到自豪。"

热爱你的工作。知名的环保作家汤姆说："我非常喜欢早上那种为做出了贡献而兴奋的感觉。如果我对某事没有激情，就绝对不会去做。否则，我为什么要做这件事? 我在阿拉巴马州还是个孩子的时候，就对户外运动产生了兴趣。在我40年左右的职业生涯中，我一直满怀这种兴趣和激情，而且从来没有改变过。在我看来，成功意味着你为生活去做一些你绝对喜欢做的事情。如果你热爱你的工作，你从中获得多少回报几乎就不重要了。"

感受工作和生活的联系。你花了多少时间进行与你的真实生活和感受不相关的活动? 许多人感觉工作不同于生活。一家技术公

interest and excitement through some 40 years of my career, and I don't see it going away. In my view, success means that you get to do something for a living that you absolutely love doing. It almost doesn't matter how much you get paid for it, if you love it."

Feel connected. How much of your time do you spend on activities that feel unconnected to your real life or feelings? Many people have the sense that work is different from life. "You work. And then when you're not working, you can live," says a 20-something rising star in a technology company.

We feel that one measure of success is how closely you feel that what you do at work expresses your highest sense of who you are. "I feel successful when I can look at my life and say that I spend most of my time doing things that feel important in some bigger sense," says Richard, a manager. "I think that as a manager, people look up to me and look to me to set the moral course for the company. I want every decision I make and every contact I have to express my deeply held values about honesty and connectedness. I don't want to look back on my life and feel that I didn't really contribute anything."

All of these people are grappling① with the question of what success means for them. In each case, it means much more than money or position. It has a lot more to do with their sense of who they are as people and the sense that their work could express that. It may really come down to the idea that success ultimately depends on getting past the easy answers of money and prestige②, and finding the more complex answers within.

(885 words)

---

① grapple [ˈgræpl] *vi.* 抓住,捉牢

② prestige [presˈtiːʒ] *n.* 威信,声望

司的一位20岁左右的后起之秀说："工作是工作。只有你不工作时，才称得上是生活。"

我们认为，你感到你做的工作是多么密切地表达了你是谁的最高境界，这是成功的一个标准。理查德经理说："当我回顾自己的生活，可以说我花了大部分时间来做我认为某种更重要的事情时，我感到很成功。我觉得作为一个经理，人们对我有所期望，指望我为公司制定道德规范。我希望自己做的每一个决定、我进行的每一次交往，都能表达我关于诚实和相互交往的根深蒂固的价值观。我不愿在回首生活时，感到自己一事无成。"

所有这些人都一直在努力思考成功对他们来说意味着什么。在每一个例子中，成功远远不只意味着金钱或地位。成功对他们有更多的意义，包括他们自身具有的价值和他们的工作能够反映的价值。这可以真正归结到这种观点，即成功最终并不是取决于金钱和声望的简单答案，而是取决于从金钱和声望之中找到更加复杂的答案。

题记

我们每个人都相伴着金钱长大,接受金钱就像接受水和空气一般自然。我们很少花时间对拥有的金钱进行心理分析——问自己希望从工作中获得什么,金钱能够为自己做些什么,或是花费在赚钱上的时间与自己的人生有何关系。钱几乎总是工作和职业生涯故事中沉默的潜台词。但当人们以钱为主题,按叙事的方式写出自己的“钱的自传”时,却有一番蓦然回首、灯火阑珊的感觉:原来我们的幸福和快乐,是如此被金钱困扰和捆绑。我们习惯用父母留下的财富为自己套上枷锁,用快速赚钱的方式来精确地衡量成功。实际上,当一个人将金钱与个人价值观相连接之后,才能真正享受到金钱带来的安全感与幸福。也许“钱的自传”能给我们一些醍醐灌顶的启发。

Money Autobiography

Pamela York Klainer advises high achievers on the challenges of work and life. But sooner or later, it all comes down to money. That is why she always urges her clients to write their "money autobiography."

As a veteran① career coach, Pamela York Klainer has encountered nearly every professional challenge under the sun. Her clients range from young entrepreneurs who are nervous about making it on their own to high-powered executives who are trying to spend more time with their families. But, she says, at the root of most such problems lies one issue: money. How much of it do people really want, and what are they prepared to give up in order to get it?

"It's considered distasteful to talk about money, and it's seen as especially distasteful to talk about our feelings about money," says Klainer, 54, who was a financial planner until 1991, when she became a career coach. In 1996, she began a "stewardship consulting" practice, which involves helping new millionaires and other people who struggle with the psychological issues that wealth raises. "But in my experience, money is almost always the silent subtext to stories about work and career."

That's why Klainer, who is based in Rochester, New York, gives

---

① veteran [ˈvɛtərən] *n.* 老手,富有经验的人

钱的自传

潘蜜拉·约克·柯莱纳给高端成功人士提供如何面对工作和生活挑战的建议，但这些建议或早或迟还是归结到钱的问题上来，这就是为什么她总是敦促客户写下他们的“钱的自传”。

作为资深的职业教练，潘蜜拉·约克·柯莱纳几乎遇到过天底下所有的职业挑战。她的客户既有忐忑不安地赚钱的年轻企业家，也有试图花更多的时间与家人相处的精力充沛的经理主管。但是她说，大多数此类问题归根到底只有一个结论：钱。人们到底需要多少钱，为了得到钱愿意付出什么代价？

柯莱纳54岁，1991年之前做财务规划师，之后成为职业规划教练。她说：“谈钱令人厌恶，可见谈论我们对金钱的感觉真使人特别反感。”1996年，她开始做“管理咨询”工作，其中包括帮助新的百万富翁和其他由于财富引起心理问题的人。“以我的经验，钱几乎总是工作和职业生涯故事中沉默的潜台词。”

这就是为什么纽约罗契斯特市的柯莱纳给客户的不寻常的任务：她要求他们以钱为主题，按叙事的方式写一份“钱的自传”，记载他们生活中的故事。他们还记得第一次有钱的感觉吗？他们在家中是怎么讨论钱的？他们能想出一个具体的形象解释钱在他们的

her clients an unusual assignment: She asks them to write a "money autobiography" — to document their life story using money as the narrative theme. When do they first remember having money of their own? How was money discussed in their family? Can they think of a concrete image that illustrates the role that money has played in their life? "A helpful way to understand your relationship to money is to tell stories about significant events in your life in which money played a part," says Klainer. "We all grow up getting certain messages about money."

Decoding① those messages — facing your hidden anxieties and expectations about money — is more important than ever, she adds, because people today have more responsibility then ever to shape their own growth. One reason why people are quick to jump at the wrong job, or even the wrong career, is that they're not honest with themselves about their material expectations: For most of us, there is a discontinuity between the story we create for ourselves and the life we want to lead.

A money autobiography helps to pinpoint② that discontinuity. The owner of a marketing firm, for instance, recently came to Klainer to express concern that she was unhappy with how hard she was working. This woman, who was in her forties, wanted to spend more time with her family — yet she was constantly pushing herself to meet high financial goals. Thanks to an inheritance from her parents, she was already worth several million dollars. But she wouldn't allow herself to touch that fortune until she had amassed③ one of her own. When Klainer asked her why, the executive seemed at a loss: "It was just a rule that she'd made for herself," Klainer says.

---

① decode [ˌdiːˈkəud] *vt.* 解码,译解

② pinpoint [ˈpinˌpɔint] *v.* 查明

③ amass [əˈmæs] *vt.* 收集,积聚(尤指财富)

生活中所扮演的角色吗？ 柯莱纳说："讲述钱在生活的重大事件中发挥的作用，是理解你和钱的关系的有效方式。 我们都伴随着钱传递的某种信息成长。"

当你面对钱流露出隐藏的焦虑和期望时，解读这些信息比以往更加重要，因为现在的人比以往更有责任来塑造自己的成长。为什么人们会在错误的工作、甚至是错误的职业中迅速跳槽，就是因为他们没有诚实地对待自己的物质欲望：对我们大多数人来说，我们为自己创造的故事和我们所想要过的生活没有连续性。

钱的自传有助于精确地描述这种非连续性。例如，一家营销公司的老板最近向柯莱纳表达了她的焦虑，她工作勤奋努力，但感觉不到快乐。 这位40岁左右的女性希望能和家人一起度过更多的时间，而她自己又不断地督促自己去达到更高的财务目标。 由于继承了父母的财产，她已有数百万美元的身家。 但她要让自己积累一笔钱之后，再去动用那笔财产。 柯莱纳问她为什么要这样做，这位经理似乎也很迷茫。 柯莱纳说："这就是一条她为自己设定的规则。"

这位经理在写她的钱的自传时，意识到她一直试图"把自己和父母相比"。 她的父母是白手起家的百万富翁。 利用遗产使自己活得更轻松似乎不是一件合理的事情。 现在，这位经理正在重新评估她强加给自己的"规则"，并考虑捐出部分财富给慈善机构。

事实上，很多客户发现，他们一直生活在父母留下的钱的规则中，而这些规则已经不适用了。 48岁的芭芭拉·摩尔也开始来见柯莱纳。 她在创办自己的互联网咨询业务两年后，产生了许多疑虑。她赚的钱足以维持她的生活方式，但她的收入低于她在罗彻斯特大学图书馆担任馆长助理时的收入。

While writing her money autobiography, this executive realized that she was trying to "measure up to her parents," who were self-made millionaires. Using an inheritance to make your life easier wasn't seen as a legitimate thing to do. Now this executive is reevaluating her self-imposed "rule" and thinking about donating some of her wealth to a charity.

In fact, many clients discover that they are living by rules about money that were handed down to them by their parents — and that no longer apply. Barbara Moore, 48, started seeing Klainer, too. Two years after she launched her own Internet-consulting business, Moore was plagued with doubts. She was earning enough to maintain her lifestyle, but her income was less than it had been when she was assistant director of libraries at the University of Rochester.

When Moore wrote her money autobiography, she began to see that she was defining success in the same way that her Depression-era parents — one a professor, the other a high-school teacher — had defined it. "To them, you always had to make more money every year, and you never quit a well-paying job," she says. With Klainer's help, Moore is rewriting her definition of success. Instead of measuring success strictly in terms of immediate dollars, she now looks at how many repeat customers and referrals① she has, at the impact that her work has on people, and at whether that work is fulfilling to her. "I still have doubts," Moore says. "But now I know where those doubts come from, and I can work on them."

(765 words)

---

① referral [riˈfəːrəl] *n.* 提名，被推举的人

摩尔在写她的钱的自传时，开始明白自己对成功的定义与生活在大萧条时期的父母对成功的定义相同。她的父母一个是教授，另一个是高中老师。她说："对他们来说，你每年总要赚更多的钱，并且从来不会辞去一份高薪工作。"在柯莱纳的帮助下，摩尔重新定义了成功。她没有用快速赚取美元的方式来精确地衡量成功，她现在更关注自己有多少回头客和被引荐的客人，关注这项工作对人们的影响，以及她做这项工作是否感到充实。摩尔说："我仍然心存困惑。但现在我知道这些疑虑来自何方，并且我可以解除这些烦恼。"

知识链接

Pamela York Klainer 潘蜜拉·约克·柯莱纳博士是美国知名的企管顾问与财富咨询大师，她的著作《你拥有多少钱才够?》主要讲述了金钱的故事，书中包含着人生的哲理和对金钱进行的心理分析，是职场新人、中级主管、自主创业者或是望着股市发愁的退休预备队的必修课。

题　记

在物欲膨胀的时代，人们渴望财富。那么，财富的尽头到底在哪里？即使是从唐人街毫无戒心的洛杉矶人手中掠夺了几百万美元财富的凶残的商业大亨诺亚·科斯，也仍然还有买不起的东西——未来。虽然整个工业的迅速增长使得那些极度富裕者纵情于他们的所有欲望，但那句古老的格言仍在昭示着一条真理：财富和快乐并无必然的联系，金钱并不是万能的。实际上，人外有人，山外有山，不管你拥有多少，总有一天会有比你拥有更多财富的人出现。人生走过的每一段路都在创造和保持一种幸福平衡的状态，借助推动力、企业家身份，成就感和社交圈通向财富的尽头；人生穿越的每一扇门都是普通人纪念之门，因为普通人是如此成功，他的不朽使他的名字与其他事物都连在了一起。

Going through the Joe Bloggs Memorial Doorway

At some point, anyone whose success or good fortune has brought them riches must wrestle with the question, "How much is enough?" For Noah Cross, the murderous tycoon who plundered① millions from unsuspecting Angelinos in Chinatown, Roman Polanski's 1974 film noir classic, only the future would do.

Most of us would be content with less but where does one draw the line? On the one hand, the soaring cost of retirement means the word "millionaire" is no longer the catch-all for wealth that it used to be. In big cities such as New York and Los Angeles, a fortune in the single-digit millions is no longer the gateway to a care free life. And on the other, even though entire industries have sprung up to help the ultra-wealthy indulge their every desire, the old adage② holds true: wealth and happiness do not necessarily go hand in hand.

Mr Cross's $ 10m fortune would have been considered remarkable in

---

① plunder [ˈplʌndə] *n.* 抢夺,战利品

② adage [ˈædidʒ] *n.* 古话,格言

穿越普通人纪念之门

在某种意义上，那些因为成功或好运带给他们财富的人必须对付这样一个难缠的话题："多少钱才是足够的？" 对诺亚·科斯来说，只有未来才知道这个问题的答案。诺亚·科斯是罗曼·波兰斯基 1974 年出品的轰动一时的黑色经典影片《唐人街》中的人物，他是一位凶残的商业大亨，从唐人街毫无戒心的洛杉矶人手中掠夺了几百万美元的巨额财富。

我们大多数人只要少许一点就会满足，但哪儿是我们的底线呢？一方面，日益猛涨的退休成本意味着"百万富翁"这个词不再是财富包罗万象的杂物袋，而人们往往对此习以为常。在像纽约和洛杉矶这样的大城市，几百万左右的财富不再是自由生活的通道。另一方面，即使整个工业的迅速增长使那些超级富豪沉溺于他们的每一个欲望，但那句古老的格言仍然昭示着一条真理：财富与幸福并无必然的联系。

在 20 世纪 40 年代洛杉矶的唐人街，科斯先生一千万美元的财产会被认为是个天文数字。但在现今，有些私有银行只与个人财产

Chinatown's 1940s Los Angeles. But today some private banks do a brisk trade dealing only with clients whose personal fortunes total $ 20m or more. They prefer to deal with those whose net worth is measured in the hundreds of millions. And although bankers are reluctant to pinpoint a new benchmark, it is clear that the term "millionaire" is fading into obsolescence① as a useful gauge② of wealth. Thanks to the increasing cost of living, and in particular the rising cost of retirement, bankers say a benchmark like $ 10m might be more appropriate for a modest fortune. If you have $ 100m in the bank, you can rest easy, and you pretty much have it made.

John Benevides, president of the Family Office Exchange, a wealth advisory group, says that, adjusting for inflation, the cost of retirement has increased more than 11-fold since the 1950s. Retirees are living longer, more active lives and healthcare costs are soaring. That is pushing the bottom rung of the wealth ladder higher, and at a faster pace than before. For example, Mr Bene-vides says a quarter of all people can expect to spend at least 18 months of their life in a nursing home. Twenty per cent will spend at least two years there. The cost of a room in a long-term care facility can average between $ 60,000 and $ 70,000 a year. Furthermore, all the planning to date has been built off actuarial③ tables that were developed at a time when people didn't live as long. The result is that even though members of the middle class drive fancier cars, and live

---

① obsolescence [ɔbsəˈlesns] *n.* 荒废,退化
② gauge [gedʒ] *n.* 标准度量,计量器
③ actuarial [æktjuˈeəriəl] *a.* 保险统计的

总额达到2 000万美元以上的客户做大宗交易。他们更喜欢和那些净资产数以亿元计的客户合作。虽然银行家不情愿制定新的基准点，但很明显，百万富翁这个词作为巨额财富的度量标准正在逐渐消失。由于生活成本上升，尤其是退休成本增加，银行认为用一千万美元作为中等财富的基准可能更适合。如果你有1亿美元的银行存款，你就可以高枕无忧，想干什么都行。

财富顾问集团的家族事务交易所的主席约翰·比勒威德斯认为，由于调整通货膨胀，退休成本自20世纪50年代以来已经增长了11倍之多。退休人员的寿命越长，生活得越有活力，卫生保健费用就会急剧增加。这就把底层劳动者的财富阶梯推得更高，并且比以往的上升速度更快。例如，比勒威德斯先生预期，四分之一的人一生中将至少在养老院度过18个月。20%的人至少会在养老院住2年的时间。长期护理中心的房间费用平均每年6万至7万美元。到目前为止，所有的计划已经建成保险精算表，预期人们会活得更久。结果表明，即使中产阶级的人开着更漂亮的汽车，住着更大的房子，消费明显比过去几年大肆增加，大量的人可能发现，他们的退休财务计划仍显不足。在财富阶梯顶层的超级富豪中，积极有效地回答“多少钱才是足够的”这个问题，需要一种更加冷静达观的态度。

一家财富管理集团谢尔特伍德金融服务公司的首席公关经理苏珊·科里说：“我见过一些只有2 000万美元而幸福生活着的人，我

in bigger homes and consume more conspicuously than in years past, a significant number may find their financial planning for retirement falls short. At the top of the ladder, among the ultra-wealthy, useful answers to the question "how much is enough" require a more philosophical approach.

"I've seen people who are blissfully satisfied with their lives at $20m and I'veseen people who are absolutely miserable at half a billion," says Suzanne Currie, chief relationship manager at Shelterwood Financial Services, a wealth management group. Ms Currie recalls that when Steve Ballmer, the chief executive of Microsoft, arrived at last year's Fort Lauderdale International Boat Show on his mammoth① yacht, The Octopus, she overheard the publisher of a yachting magazine scoff. "He said: 'You know, you really are nobody unless you have a full-sized basketball court on the back of your boat'." For Ms Currie, the incident underlined an important lesson. "No matter how much you think you have achieved, there is always someone with more."

Mary Duke, a managing director at HSBC private bank, says the temptation to measure one's own success against that of others can lead to trouble. "There is a greed factor, and I think it is very important people disassociate from it," she says. "It is a vicious cycle and it is an unwinnable game. If you are looking for happiness by owning the biggest yacht that pulls into the harbor, you are probably going down an unpleasant alley." Wealth doesn't make you happy and it doesn't self-

---

① mammoth [ˈmæməθ] *a.* 巨大的

也见过一些拥有5 000万美元却痛苦不堪的人。”科里回忆到，当微软的首席执行官史蒂夫·巴尔默带着他庞大的游艇章鱼号参加去年的罗德岱堡国际游艇展时，她无意中听到一家游艇杂志的出版人嘲弄史蒂夫。“他说：‘你要清楚，除非你的船后部有一个标准尺寸的篮球场，否则你就没什么好炫耀的’。”对科里来说，这件事给了她深刻的启示：“人外有人，山外有山。”

汇丰私人银行的常务董事玛丽·杜克认为，拿自己的成功与他人的成功比较是自讨麻烦。她说：“贪婪是诱因，我认为，关键是让人们远离贪婪。它是一个恶劣循环，是一场无法取胜的游戏。如果你想利用拥有进入港口的最大游艇来寻找幸福，你很可能走向一条没有快乐的小道。”财富不能使人快乐，也不能实现自我价值。人类的议题与财富没有什么实质联系。他们可能因财富而喧哗，也可能因财富而沉默。杜克认为，“最重要的事是确保收支平衡。假定你的收入远超过了支出，假定客户有足够的财富度日，那么我们所有客户的首要问题是他们的孩子。他们应该把留给孩子的财产和他们生命中的成功前景联系起来”。

当然，财富也不是万能药。“含着金钥匙”长大的人能给孩子提供各种他人无法获得的经验和机会，但同时也存在自身的弊端。一些经济上成功的人士最终转向慈善事业，将自己赚的大部分钱财回馈给社会。少数人不再采用签支票这种传统模式投资这个有价值的事业，而是投入自己的时间、劳力和技能，支持自己最喜欢的

actualize. The human issues have nothing to do with wealth. They might be accentuated① by wealth or muted by wealth. "The most important thing is making sure you live within your means. Assuming you are well beyond that and assuming the client has wealth to live off, the number one issue all our clients have is their children," Duke says. "They make a link between the wealth they can hand off to them for success in life."

Here, too, wealth is not a panacea②. Growing up a member of the "lucky gene pool" may provide children with a variety of experiences and opportunities not available to others but it creates problems of its own. Some financially successful people eventually turn to philanthropy as an outlet for making the most of what they have achieved. A few have begun to move beyond the traditional model of writing a cheque to a worthy cause to lend their own time, labour and skills to their favourite causes.

These are useful outlets. But in the end, says Ms Currie, there are five things people want. It's the drive, the entrepreneurship, it's the achievement, and it's welcoming yourself into what you perceive as the social circle you'd like to be in. The fifth item is immortality. All you have to do is go to any university campus. Every doorway you go through is the Joe Bloggs③ memorial doorway, because Joe Bloggs has become so successful that his immortality is having his name attached to something.

(957 words)

---

① accentuate [æk'sentjueit] *v.* 以重音念，强调
② panacea [ˌpænə'siə] *n.* 万灵药
③ Joe Bloggs *n.* 普通的人，老百姓

事业。

这些都是有益的支出。科里女士认为，人们最终想做五件事，它们分别是推动力、企业家身份、成就感以及希望自己能加入所喜爱的社交圈。第五件是不朽的名声，你需要做的就是走进任何一所大学校园。你穿越的每一扇门都是普通人纪念之门，因为普通人是如此成功，他的不朽使他的名字与其他事物连在了一起。

知识链接

Fort Lauderdale International Boat Show 罗德岱堡国际游艇展。美国佛罗里达州的罗德岱堡国际游艇展号称是世界上最大的游艇展，每年十月在罗德岱堡举行。来自世界各地的游艇制造商在游艇展上展出各式游艇、发动机以及成千种游艇配件。整个展会设有水陆展区，面积超过300多万平方英尺，各展区间可通过水上的士、内河船及巴士连接。

HSBC 汇丰集团（The Hongkong and Shanghai Banking Corporation Limited）是全球规模最大的银行及金融机构之一，在欧洲、亚太地区、美洲、中东及非洲76个国家和地区拥有约9 500间附属机构，提供广泛的银行及金融服务：个人金融服务、工商业务、企业银行、投资银行及资本市场、私人银行以及其他业务。

题　记

人类与生俱来的悲观主义，让他们面对突如其来的财富时保持一种审慎的态度。数百万欧元的彩票赢家多洛雷斯·麦克纳马拉一夜之间名声大振，成为国家新的财富和安全忧患的符号，却让更多的公众开始迫切希望找到金钱根本不会使你幸福的证据。当一度被视为奢侈标准的收入现在已经习以为常、而被认为留给富豪的财产已经完全大众化之时，人类却跌入了需要更高的工资、更多的加班、上下班往返时间更长以及降低支出和价值之间的平衡期望值的黑暗空间。一旦人的基本需求得到满足，幸福指数的变化随着数百万财富的积累，也会受到收益递减规律的支配。所以，低调的消费才能珍惜你获得的祝福：健康是开启财富之门的钥匙；家庭是获取财富的强大后盾；朋友是扶助财富增长的智慧；你喜欢做的工作会给你赢得财富的过程带来最大的快乐。好好珍惜、用心守护人生中获得的各种祝福，直到有一天，你发现自己也成了一位富翁。

Counting Your Blessings

It was hard to avoid those pictures of Dolores McNamara, the Euromillions lottery winner, splashed all over the tabloids① during the week. Leaving her mother's funeral, McNamara was photographed crying in the front seat of a large Mercedes. As news stories go, it wasn't earth-shattering. The loss of a parent is something most normal folk tend to find upsetting. But maybe the tabloid editors were trying to make a different point. McNamara has more than €100m in the bank, so pictures of her looking blissfully happy equal no news. Pictures of rich-as-Croesus② Dolores looking miserable — now that's something.

It seems the Limerick lottery winner has come to represent a 21st-century version of Mother Macree, the country's spirit embodied in a female form. The French have Marianne, their symbol of liberty, equality and fraternity. We have Dolores, emblem of new wealth, instant celebrity and security worries. Not long ago she was poor, now she's rich. Outside her circle she was unknown, living on an estate in the suburbs of an unloved city. Now she's famous, coiffed and courted and free to move in

---

① tabloid [ˈtæblɔid] *n.* 小报,药片
② Croesus [ˈkriːsəs] *n.* 大富豪,大财主

珍惜你获得的祝福

数百万欧元的彩票赢家多洛雷斯·麦克纳马拉的照片本周占满了各种小报的版面，想不看都难。麦克纳马拉刚离开母亲的葬礼，就被拍到坐在一辆豪华奔驰车的前排号啕大哭。作为新闻故事报道，这本不是什么惊天动地的事件。普通人失去父母伤心欲绝是再正常不过的事了。但是，小报的编辑们正试图编出不同的噱头。麦克纳马拉已有 1 亿多欧元的银行存款，所以她看上去幸福快乐的照片就不算新闻了。大富豪一般的多洛雷斯从照片上看可怜兮兮——这就很特别了。

看来这位利默里克彩票得主能够代表 21 世纪的慈母形象——以女性形象表达的国家精神。法国人有玛丽安，她是自由、平等和博爱的象征。我们有多洛雷斯，她是新的财富、一夜成名和安全忧患的符号。不久前，她还是穷人，但现在她是富豪。她过去在自己的生活圈子之外默默无闻，住在不受人喜爱的市郊。现在她名声大振，戴着压发帽，搬进了带庭院的豪宅，自由出入顶级的社交名流圈。她曾是一个普通人，和其他无数人一样勉强维持生计。现在她富甲一方，人人都想成为她的朋友，她开始小心谨慎地接触圈

the most glittering circles. She was an ordinary soul, struggling like countless others to make ends meet. Now she's loaded and everyone wants to be her friend, so she's got to be careful who she admits to her circle.

The parallels with modern-day Ireland are striking — small wonder, then, that there appears to be huge public appetite for evidence that money doesn't make you happy, after all. It's something we are just beginning to suspect ourselves. New figures released indicate that most of us are earning much more than ever before. The Department of Finance, possibly with an eye to the budget, has been amassing evidence that we have money to burn — or money for the Exchequer to burn.

Only several years ago, at what was considered the height of the Celtic tiger boom, no more than 100 employees in the PAYE regime earned in excess of € 1m a year. The new figures show that three times that number will have topped the € 1m mark now. More than 50,000 workers will earn more than € 100,000 this year — almost four times greater than before. In other words, incomes that were once regarded as luxury level are now commonplace and acquisitions that were considered the preserve of the very lucky or the very rich are now positively vulgar. So you'vegot yourself a holiday home? That will be you and 599,999 others. Even Dolores had one before she won the jackpot.

The World Database of Happiness is a project devised by the University of Erasmus in the Netherlands. It published a global survey in which citizens of 90 countries rated their enjoyment of life on a scale of 1 to 10. We came in joint second, alongside Iceland and behind Denmark, Malta and Switzerland. The Danes, Maltese and Swiss rated their general contentment at 8 out of 10, while we ranked ours at 7. 8. The research

里人。

与当代的爱尔兰相提并论的确引人注目，但有点小意外，似乎大量的公众迫切希望找到金钱根本不会使你幸福的证据。这正是我们为什么开始怀疑自己的原因。新公布的数据显示，我们大多数人的收入远远超过以往任何时候。盯着收支预算的财政部，可能已经收集了大量的证据，说明我们有用不完的钱，或者说国库有用不完的钱。

就在几年前，即凯尔特虎经济繁荣的鼎盛时期，在预扣政府所得税的体制中，每年超过100万欧元收入的雇员还不到100名。新的数据显示，现在收入超过百万欧元的员工数目是此前的三倍。5万多名工人今年的收入将超过10万欧元，这几乎是以前的四倍。换句话说，曾一度被视为奢侈标准的收入现在已经习以为常，而被认为留给非常幸运或非常富有的人的财产已经完全大众化。你给自己买了度假住地吗？这就是你和其他599 999人同样享有的权利。即使是多洛雷斯，在她赢得大奖之前也是其中一位。

世界幸福数据库是荷兰伊拉斯谟大学设计的一个项目。它发布的一份全球调查中，将90个国家的公民快乐生活指数按1至10评级。我们与冰岛并列第二，排在丹麦、马耳他和瑞士之后。丹麦、马耳他和瑞士的满意度选择一般是10分之8，但我们只有7.8。这项调查完成时，我们所有人正在开始感受经济繁荣的好处，给自己买00牌照的车、时髦的手机和美式冰箱。随着时间的流逝，我们从“敲共和国的竹杠”这一档电视节目秀中醒来，认识

for the survey was done about the time when we were all beginning to feel the benefits of the boom, buying ourselves 00-reg cars, swanky① mobile phones and American-style fridge-freezers. As time goes on, we'vewoken up in Rip-Off Republic and realized that the fancy mobile, the big car and the designer kitchen don't count for much when everybody else has them. We are also discovering that sustaining status requires ever-higher wages, more overtime, longer commutes and lower expectations of any equation between outlay and value.

Our incomes on paper have tripled in the years since that research was carried out, but it's unlikely we'd rate our happiness level at anything like 8 out of 10 these days. Money makes you happy up to a point, but numerous surveys of the wealthy have established that, once a human's basic needs are met, the changes in your happiness levels as you notch up② the millions is governed by the law of diminishing returns. Once you tick the boxes for food and shelter, security and love, self-esteem and fulfilment, there is no extrinsic source of joy that money can introduce to your life. And not only are all of these factors achievable on a relatively modest income but, according to people who study these things, superfluous wealth and acquisition can actually make you unhappy.

In a high-income economy, your happiness doesn't just hinge on how you spend your money — it's equally dependent on what others do. Professor Robert Frank of Cornell University, the author of Luxury Fever,

---

① swanky [ˈswæŋki] *adj.* 奢华的,豪华的

② notch up 完成,创下

到当每个人都拥有华丽的手机、豪车和精心设计的厨房时，这一切犹如过眼烟云。我们还正在发现，维持现状需要更高的工资、更多的加班、上下班往返时间更长以及降低支出和价值之间的平衡期望值。

自从这项研究实施以来，我们的收入几年中翻了三番，但不幸的是，我们的幸福指数现在仍然没有达到10分之8。在某种程度上，金钱能给你带来幸福，但对富人的多项调查已经表明，一旦人的基本需求得到满足，幸福指数的变化随着数百万财富的积累，也会受到收益递减规律的支配。一旦你需要在食物和住所、安全感和爱情、自尊和成就之间做出选择，金钱并不是给你的生活带来外在快乐的源泉。只有相对适中的收入才能满足所有的这些因素，根据研究人员的观点，过剩的财富和财产其实并不会使你感到幸福。

在高收入经济时期，你的幸福不仅仅取决于如何花钱，同样依赖于他人的行为。康奈尔大学的罗伯特·弗兰克教授，是《奢侈品发烧友》的作者，他把我们这样的挥霍性消费比作军事军备竞赛，而我们已经知道，我们将注定面临两败俱伤的结局。假设你买了一辆带防撞架的超大吉普，与开着只有10年历史的“小星”车驾驶者相撞，你在车祸中活下来的机会更大。当然，除非其他每个人都开着一辆带防撞架的大吉普，那么，你希望用6万欧元买来的内心宁静会急剧贬值。不幸的是，你并不适合开悍马。时尚的百货公司里，滑稽而昂贵的名牌服装店铺天盖地，远距离度假和活动广受欢迎，用战利品雕饰的住宅成本上涨，这一切都意味着，我们衡量物

compares conspicuous consumption in an economy like ours to the military arms race, and we already know that's destined to end in mutually assured destruction. Say you buy a really big Jeep with bull bars①. You have a better chance of surviving a crash than the guy in the 10-year-old Starlet, unless, of course, everyone else is driving a big Jeep with bull bars. So the peace of mind you'd hoped to buy for € 60,000 has been hugely devalued. Unfortunately, a Hummer won't fit in your drive. The mushrooming of ludicrously expensive designer clothes outlets in swish② department stores, the popularity of distant holiday destinations and activities, and the rising cost of trophy③ homes all mean the bar against which we measure our material success is rising without any commensurate④ improvement in our levels of contentment.

Most of all, inconspicuous consumption is about counting your blessings — health, family, friends, a job you like even if it doesn't set the world on fire — rather than costing and envying and trying to match those of others. And if it's any consolation, research has shown that within a year of a big lottery jackpot, the winner's happiness returns to its previous level. Admit it: that's just what you wanted to hear. So let's give Dolores a break.

(974 words)

---

① bull bars 护架,防撞架

② swish[swiʃ] *adj.* 好看的,时髦的

③ trophy [ˈtrəufi] *n.* 战利品

④ commensurate [kəˈmenʃərit] *adj.* 相等的,相称的

质成功的标准正在升高，但我们的满意程度却没有任何相应的改善。

总之，低调的消费才能珍惜你获得的祝福，它们分别是健康、家庭、朋友、你喜欢做的工作——即使它并不是惊天动地的大事，而不是斤斤计较、嫉妒以及试图与他人攀比。研究表明，在一年之内，彩票头奖大赢家的幸福感会返回到以前的水平，不知道这是不是个安慰。承认这一点：这就是你所想听到的。所以，让我们放多洛雷斯一马吧。

知识链接

Mother Machree 《慈母》是导演约翰·福特在1928年拍摄的一步无声影片，讲述了一位贫穷的爱尔兰移民母亲的故事。Machree一词在爱尔兰语中表示"宝贝儿，心肝"的亲昵意思。

PAYE 所得税预扣法(Pay As You Earn)。预扣所得税又叫withholding tax是指雇主替政府从职员薪资中扣缴的所得税。因为如果政府要对一般纳税人逐一收税，难度很大，而且没有保证，如果企业直接从职工的工资中扣掉所得税再把它交给国家，这样可以很好地避免偷税漏税现象。

The Celtic Tiger 凯尔特虎。爱尔兰民族是凯尔特人的后裔，所以在欧洲通常被称为"凯尔特虎"。此处是对爱尔兰经济快速增长的赞誉。

Starlet "小星"是丰田公司竞争力已明显不足的一种老车型。现在这种车型已被新款取代。

题　记

“金钱”是我们这个时代一个响亮的名词。政治家们理直气壮地谈论金钱，因为希腊、冰岛的债务危机使他们筋疲力尽、治国无门；商界精英津津乐道地谈论金钱，因为他们害怕房利美、房地美、雷曼兄弟之类的灭顶之灾再次向他们袭来。普通老百姓对金钱过度痴迷，早上起床的第一件事是打开收音机，收听关于期货交易的讨论或股票交易市场夜间的交易表现；白天收看电视新闻，眼睛会盯着屏幕角落里浮动显示的道琼斯工业指数。过去不是这样。传统的宗教、哲学和道德摆出一副道貌岸然、正人君子的架势，将金钱打入万恶之源的十八层地狱，谴责财富给人类和社会造成的恶果。一般俗人即使喜欢财富，也羞于声张，当众谈钱也会感到尴尬。其实，公开讴歌金钱，是资本主义造就的一种新观念：一方面把获取金钱作为人生的重要成就予以鼓励，另一方面又要求节制物质享受的欲望。

Avoiding Talking about Money

There was a time when Americans didn't talk about money. It's true. Money went unmentioned in polite conversation.

Hard to believe, because money is all people talk about now. Bailouts①, mortgage-backed securities, cramdowns, liquidity, Fannie Mae, Freddie Mac, AIG, Lehman Brothers, Citi and on and on. The U.S. obsession with money is everywhere you turn. Tap on the radio first thing in the morning, and there's talk of futures trading and how the Tokyo Stock Exchange fared overnight. Watch daytime news on CNN and you can't avoid the vacillating② Dow Jones industrial average in the corner of your screen. A score of international leaders met in Washington recently to discuss — money.

"We never talked about money in our family when I was growing up," says Deena Katz, 58, professor of personal finance at Texas Tech University. Katz says she only got interested in money and investments when her father died and her mother needed help in financial matters.

---

① bailout [ˈbeilaut] *n.* (公司所受的)紧急援助

② vacillating [ˈvæsileitiŋ] *adj.* 犹豫的,踌躇的

逃避谈钱

曾经有一段时间，美国人不愿意谈论金钱。这是真的。在礼貌的谈话中，不会有人提到金钱。

这很难让人相信，因为金钱现在是所有人都在谈论的话题。紧急援助措施、抵押贷款支持的证券、强制执行的计划、流动资金、房利美、房地美、美国国际集团、雷曼兄弟、花旗银行，等等。无论到哪你都会发现，美国对金钱过度痴迷。美国人早上的第一件事是打开收音机，收听关于期货交易的讨论以及东京股票交易市场夜间的交易表现。白天收看美国有线电视新闻网的新闻时，美国人的眼睛会盯着屏幕角落里浮动显示的道琼斯工业指数。最近，二十几位国际领导人在华盛顿举行会晤，中心议题就是金钱。

58 岁的德克萨斯理工大学个人理财教授蒂娜·卡兹说："在我成长的过程中，从未在家中谈过钱。"卡兹表示，父亲去世后母亲需要钱花时，她才开始对钱和投资感兴趣。《金钱》杂志的创刊主编威廉·S. 鲁凯赛认为，半个世纪前，人们从来不讨论金钱的话题，现在，这个话题已经变成公开场合的正常谈资。的确，上流社会很久

William S. Rukeyser, the founding editor of Money magazine, says that a half-century ago, people avoided talking about money, but now the subject has become fair game for parlor conversation. To be sure, the upper crust has long whispered of wealth at country clubs and Upper East Side cocktail parties. And magazines for the rich such as Fortune and Forbes were around for much of the 20th century. But it wasn't until the later part of the 20th century that most middle-class Americans began throwing "money" around — the word, not the currency.

Family incomes were spiraling①, up 85 percent adjusted for inflation, and Americans suddenly had more money to spend. And more money to fret② about — tax strategies for corporate workers, and individual retirement accounts for self-employed individuals. And then came the big shift: Large U.S. corporations moved from defined benefit, or pension, plans to defined contribution plans. Up until then, Katz says, you worked for a company for 30 years, and then you got a gold watch and a fixed retirement income. You knew exactly how much you would be receiving for the rest of your life, but you had no say in how the money was invested.

Congress opened the door for 401(k) plans, and employees began participating in retirement accounts that received their — and their employers — contributions. Soon everyone was seeking financial advice. "We were responsible for our own financial future," says Katz. As

① spiral [ˈspaiərəl] *vi.* 成螺旋形上升

② fret [fret] *vi.* (使某人)不愉快,烦躁

以来就在乡间俱乐部和上东区的鸡尾酒会上窃窃私语地讨论财富。《财富》、《福布斯》等杂志在20世纪的大部分时间里是富人的专属品。直到20世纪晚期，大多数美国中产阶级才开始大把花“钱”，这个单词的意思不是流通货币。

当家庭收入呈螺旋式上升、通货膨胀后调整到85%时，美国人突然有更多的钱花。更多的钱也让人感到焦虑不安，如公司员工们的税务策略，如何为自主经营的个体建立个人退休金账户等。接下来发生了一个重大变化：大型美国公司将固定福利或养老金转入养老金的固定缴款计划。卡兹说，从那时开始，你为一家公司工作30年，就可以得到一个金表和一份固定的退休收入。你能准确知道退休以后最终能拿多少钱，但你无权知晓钱是怎么投资的。

国会通过了401(k)计划后，雇员们开始参加退休账户，账户由雇员和雇主共同缴纳资金。很快，所有人开始寻求财政建议。卡兹认为，“我们要为自己的长期融资负责”。随着市场的沉浮，雇员的养老金储蓄随之膨胀或者缩水。人们认识到，他们应该比投资顾问更关心自己的钱。他们意识到，任何东西都不可能万无一失。

在这段婴儿潮一代崛起的时期，被称为雅皮士的年轻人是社会经济地位上升的职业人士。或许首位在电视上妙语连珠地谈论金钱的人是威廉的兄长路易斯·鲁凯泽，他的《华尔街周刊》举办的表演会上，首次让金钱荣登美国公共广播公司的大雅之堂。路易斯·鲁凯泽是一名伟大的演说家，他说话一语双关，诙谐幽默，用极具

markets rose or fell, employees, nest eggs① expanded or shriveled. People recognized they have to care more about their money than their advisers do. They realized that nothing is for sure anymore.

This was the rise of the baby boom generation — and young upwardly mobile professionals, known as yuppies. Perhaps the first person on TV to make talking about money cool was Louis Rukeyser — William's brother — whose show Wall Street Week debuted on PBS stations. Louis Rukeyser was the great demystifier②. Using punny humor and wry③ examples, he explained the arcane world of finance, with its foggy phrases such as "selling short" and "buying on margin," to the newly empowered personal investor. William Rukeyser followed in his brother's footsteps with the launch of Money magazine — an offshoot of Time. "The name 'Money, was thought by some to be incredibly crass and startling," William Rukeyser, 69, says today. In fact, when one staff member said she would be embarrassed to be caught reading a magazine called Money on the subway, Rukeyser suggested she hide it behind a copy of a lewd magazine.

The national newspaper USA Today appeared on newsstands with its four color-coded sections: News, sports, life and Money. Also in the early days, Financial News network was born and eventually was available on more than 3,000 cable systems, with a potential audience of 35

---

① nest egg 为养老而准备的钱

② demystify [diː'mistifai] *vt.* 使非神秘化

③ wry [rai] *adj.* 歪曲的

讽刺、辛辣意味的例子，解释了金融这个晦涩难解的世界，用“卖空”和“边际购买”之类的模糊词组，吸引了有实力的新生代个人投资者。威廉·鲁凯泽追随其兄的后尘，发行了《金钱》杂志，即《泰晤士报》的一份下属杂志。69岁的威廉现在说，“有些人认为，‘金钱’这个名称不可思议的粗鲁且令人震惊”。事实上，当一名职员告诉他，如果坐地铁时被人发现在看名为《金钱》的杂志时，她会感到尴尬，鲁凯泽当即建议她把杂志放在一本色情杂志的后面。

面向全国发行的大型日报《今日美国》以四个彩色的版面出现在报摊上：新闻、体育、生活和金钱。美国民众最终可用3 000多个有线电视系统收看的《金融时报》网在早些时候诞生，其潜在观众达3 500万户。《消费者新闻》和《商业频道（CNBC）》也相继问世。而“今日杂志网站”则提供180多份商业和金融杂志的订阅。

《金钱》杂志在20世纪80年代蓬勃发展的股票市场异军突起。当时还是《财富》杂志编辑的鲁凯泽认为，“我创造了一种职业，用人们希望的平实语言谈论财政问题”。当提及人们自己的金钱时，鲁凯泽认为，他的兄长将其用于周五晚间节目是明智的选择。他说：“每周谈论一次钱的问题对你考虑你的投资计划已经足够了。没有什么比每天看一小时的股市、每天思考你需要做些什么更危险了。那样做你肯定富不起来。”

卡兹进一步建议，只需要每季度一次或每年一次考虑你的投

million households. The Consumer News and Business Channel, CNBC, was launched. Today, Magazines.com offers subscriptions to more than 180 Business and finance magazines.

Money magazine boomed in the 1980s as the stock market skyrocketed. "I have made a career of trying to talk about financial matters to people in the plain language they deserve," says Rukeyser, who also was an editor at Fortune for a while. When it comes to talking about one's own money, Rukeyser believes his brother had it right with his Friday night show. "Once a week is plenty often enough to consider your investments," he says. "There is nothing more dangerous than watching the stock market every hour of every day and thinking you need to do something. That's a guaranteed route to poverty."

Going a step further, Katz suggests thinking about your investments only once a quarter or once a year. And she doesn't see the need for so much money talk. "There is a lot of financial information available," she says. "But information is not knowledge or judgment or empathy①." Investing should be like watching paint dry — it may be boring, but clients should stick with the tried and true asset classes, she adds. You should invest in solid enterprises and only make changes if there are changes in your life — like children or retirement. "You only have one life," she says. "You don't want to spend it obsessing about money."

(869 words)

---

① empathy [ˈempəθi] *n.* 移情作用,神入

资。她认为没有必要过多谈钱。她说："有很多渠道获取金融信息。但是信息既不是知识、也不是判断或同情。"她还补充说，投资应当像是等待涂料干燥的过程——可能很乏味，但客户应当坚持投资已被事实证明可靠的资产类别。你应该投资可靠的企业，只有当你的生活发生了改变时，如生子或退休，再做出相应的调整。她声称："人的生命只有一次。不要被金钱困扰。"

知识链接

USA Today 《今日美国》于1982年创刊，是美国第一份面向全国发行的大型日报。在其问世不足两年的时间里，发行量即跃至全美第三位，与《纽约时报》和《华尔街日报》这两份在读者中深入人心的百年老报并驾齐驱。《今日美国》的宗旨是要适应美国人日常生活的快节奏，迎合读者通过形象的方法获取信息的习惯，追求信息利用便捷的"快餐文化"，保持彩色印刷和大图片的鲜明特点。因此，《今日美国》也被美国人称为"报纸中的电视"。

题记

我们身处其中的微妙世界，为我们揭开了财富宇宙意识的面纱，即人内在无限大的力量源泉——内心的力量。拿破仑利用内心的力量颠覆了整个欧洲；爱因斯坦利用内心的力量发现了相对论；乔布斯利用内心的力量创造了互联网时代的苹果奇迹。我们利用内心的力量，与宇宙意识融为一体，就可以加入到创造并征服财富的能量之中。宇宙意识是无限的，也包含着无限的财富。如果我们期待通过万物来表达自己，就不仅需要创造金钱和资产，还要创造包括爱、同情、善良、力量、能量、知识和智慧等在内的多种生命形式。但是，消极的想法和态度妨碍了宇宙意识的自然倾向，使之无法自由自在地以无限的方式表达它的创造力。财富的宇宙意识改变了我们的生活，它使我们的精神不再受环境的约束和限制，它使我们的视野更开阔、思想更自由，它使我们利用与时俱进的内在力量去创造更多的财富。

Universal Consciousness of Wealth

The word wealth brings into the mind thoughts about riches, plenty of money and the ability to buy and enjoy whatever one wants. It brings thoughts about fancy houses, hotels, world travel, cars and everything money can buy. It is something most people want, but do not believe they can get and enjoy.

Wealth is all the above and much more. It is not restricted only to money and possessions. It manifests as plentitude① in various and many forms in our life and in nature. A person can be wealthy with love, compassion, goodness, strength, energy, knowledge and wisdom. Nature manifests wealth in the many life forms and plants it produces, and in the endless stars and worlds it has created. The Life Force, which is also called the Universal Consciousness, Spirit or Creative Power, desires to constantly express and manifest itself, and it does so through the physical frame of plants, animals and human beings. This power also expresses its desire to manifest wealth, which is the desire to grow, develop and become stronger and bigger. Yet, many find this desire and natural tendency for growth inhibited in them, due to negative

① plentitude [ˈplentitjuːd] *n.* 充分

财富的宇宙意识

财富这个词给人的印象是财产、大量的钱、有能力购买和享受你想要的任何东西。它让人联想到精致的房子、旅馆、环游世界、汽车以及一切用金钱可以买到的东西。这是大多数人想要但却不敢相信自己可以得到或享有的东西。

财富是前面所提及的东西或者更多，它不只是限于金钱和资产。它在我们的生活和自然界中的表现五花八门，形式各异。人因为爱、同情、善良、力量、能量、知识和智慧而富有。自然以多种生命的形式、它产生的植物、它创造的无数星星和世界来展示财富。而“生命力”，也被称为“宇宙意识、精神或创造力”，期望不断地表达和展示自己，它通过植物、动物和人类的物理形式完成自我实现。这种能量也表现了它展现财富的欲望——一种培育、发展、并越来越强大的欲望。然而，由于消极的规划、消极的想法、对自己和自己的能力缺乏信心，很多人发现这种欲望和自然倾向制约了自身的发展。

要想在生活中做到财源滚滚的第一步就是改变你对它的看法和

programming, negative thinking and lack of faith in themselves and their abilities.

The first step to make wealth flow into your life is to change your thoughts and attitude toward it. The mind has to be cleared from its wrong concepts about wealth, before it can start to manifest. This is done by bringing to consciousness all of your thoughts and ideas about wealth, money and prosperity. Take a pen and a sheet of paper, and find a place to be alone and undisturbed for a while. Think about wealth and what it means to you, and then jot① down any thought that comes into your mind. Write down every thought, good and bad, positive and negative. Do this for at least ten minutes or until you do not find more ideas and thoughts. After you finish writing, read, think, and analyze what you have written. You will be surprised at the stuff that comes out of your mind. This analysis will help you to find out where and why you are inhibiting yourself in regard to success, money, and prosperity. You will find out what thoughts and wrong concepts have been holding you back.

You will discover the fears that have been holding you from success, and from manifesting any degree of riches in your life. There might be various reasons to account for that. You may have been educated to regard wealth as bad and corrupting. You may have experienced lack in your childhood, and now you are locked into② the belief that it is not possible to improve your life or that you do not deserve to possess money. It might be that you shun③ the responsibility and the work that wealth might entail.

---

① jot [dʒɔt] *v.* 匆匆记下

② lock into 受困于

③ shun [ʃʌn] *vt.* 避开,规避

态度。在财富开始现身之前，头脑中首先要清除对财富的错误概念。做到这些需要你意识到你对财富、金钱和成功的所有思想和理念。拿出笔和纸，独自找个地方待一会，不受打扰。想想财富，以及它对你意味着什么，然后草草记下出现在你脑海中的任何想法。写下每一个想法，好的和坏的、积极的和消极的。至少坚持10分钟，或者直到你找不到更多的主意和想法。写完之后，阅读、思考并分析你写的东西。你会对大脑的所思所想感到惊奇。这种分析有助于你发现，你在哪方面以及为什么会在追求成功、金钱和富裕时禁锢自己。你会发现是什么想法和错误观念使你踌躇不前。

你会发现一直在阻止你追求成功和展现生活富裕程度的恐惧感。这种现象可以用各种各样的原因来解释。你接受的教育视财富为邪恶和腐败。你可能经历了财富匮乏的童年，现在仍难以相信财富可能改变你的生活，或者自己根本就不值得拥有金钱。或许你在逃避财富必须承担的责任和义务；或许你在担心你不会处置财富；或许你不知道如何与财富相处。这些原因或任何其他的原因，都会使你不愿体验成功和财富。内在的禁锢主要归结于以前心理上的原因，使你觉得和认为自己不配，不配成功，或者应该逃避财富和金钱。

如果你诚恳地做这种分析，就会发现是何种思维和态度阻碍了你成功的道路，你会更清楚自己要做什么。既然这些东西都已经公开，处理这些禁锢、将自己从这些禁锢中释放出来并开始吸引财富

Maybe you are afraid that you would not be able to handle wealth or that you will not know what to do with it. These reasons or any others might be responsible not experiencing prosperity and wealth. The inner inhibitions are mostly due to former mental programming, making you feel and believe that you are not worthy, do not deserve success or that wealth and money should be avoided.

If you perform this analysis sincerely, you will find out what thoughts and attitudes hinder your way to success, and it will be clearer to you what you should do. Now that they are out, it will be easier to handle these inhibitions, free yourself from their grip, and to start attracting wealth into your life. If one session is not enough, keep writing down your thoughts, and think about them every day until feel you have discovered what is holding you back.

After this analysis you will find it easier to start changing your thoughts and attitude towards money, possessions and wealth. You will find it easier, and experience less inner resistance when you visualize what you want to get or accomplish. It will take less effort to refuse negative or contradictory thoughts from entering your mind. Persistence in your efforts of holding an image of success in your mind until you realize your desire, and at the same time keeping an open mind for opportunities will lead you to do the right thing at the right time, and attract the right people at the right time.

An intense and concentrated thought possesses a vast power. All wealthy people focus their energies in a positive and powerful manner on what they desire to achieve. Some of them understand and practice consciously the laws of success, while others do so unconsciously. The

进入你的生活就会更容易。如果一个时段不够，请继续写下你的想法，每天思考这些问题，直到你发现是什么拖你的后腿。

完成这些分析之后，你会发现，改变你对金钱、财产和财富的想法和态度开始变得更加容易。当你想要得到或完成的东西形象化之后，你会发现事情更加容易，内在的禁锢感减少，将消极或矛盾的想法拒之脑外不再花费更大的力气。努力坚持在大脑中保持成功的形象，直到你意识到自己的愿望，同时保持开阔的眼界寻找机会，这将使你能够在正确的时候做正确的事，在正确的时候结交正确的朋友。

活跃的思维和全神贯注拥有巨大的能量。所有的富人都以一种积极和强势的风格，集中精力实现自己的愿望。他们中的一些人有意识地理解和践行成功的法则，而其他人却呈现一种无意识的状态。宇宙意识是无限的，也包含着无限的财富。这种意识包含很多的东西，而且不断地创造更多的东西。它通过万物来表达自己，包括你认为的自我这种个体。但问题是，消极的想法和态度妨碍宇宙意识的自然倾向，使之无法自由自在地以无限的方式表达它的创造力。

您需要开阔视野，摒弃那些局限性的想法。不管现在的生活和环境多么受限，如果选择改变你的想法和态度，开始自由地思考，你的生活将会发生改变。不要在精神上受环境的约束和限制。思考可能性，而不是限制性。拓展你无限的想象力，思考你自己、你

Universal Consciousness is unlimited and contains unlimited wealth. There is plenty of everything in it, and it constantly creates more of everything. It expresses itself through everything, including the individual unit that you consider as yourself. The problem is that negative thoughts and attitudes hamper the natural tendency of the Universal Consciousness to freely manifest its creative powers in unlimited ways.

You need to open your mind to prosperity and throw away your limiting thoughts. It does not matter how limited your life and circumstances are at the present moment, because if you choose to change your thoughts and attitudes, and start thinking without imposing limitations, your life will start to change. In your mind, refuse to be tied and limited by your circumstances. Think about possibilities, not about limitations. Expand your unlimited thinking to what you consider as yourself, your personality and individuality. Your Consciousness is one with the Universal Consciousness. If you consider yourself as only a body you limit yourself. You are limitless consciousness, but erroneously identify yourself with the body and therefore feel limited. The feeling of limitation obstructs you from expressing the great powers of the Universal Consciousness. By being one with the Universal Consciousness you participate in the power of creation. Think about it, you are connected to the powers of the Universe.

(1,004 words)

的性格和个性。你的意识和宇宙意识连为一体。如果你认为自己只是一个实体，那你就限制了自己。如果你不受思维的限制，却错误地将自己定义为一个实体，所以还是受到了限制。这种制约感阻碍了你表达宇宙意识的强大力量。与宇宙意识融为一体，你就加入到创造的能量中。想想看，你和宇宙的能量相连了。

知识链接

Universal Consciousness 宇宙意识。宇宙意识又称为生命力(First Life)、精神(Spirit)、创造力(Creative Power)。宇宙意识认为宇宙——包括人们的三维空间——的建造材料是同一的。世界、恒星、星云、太阳系统启动于一个原一起因，均是能量及振动，由于形式和波长不同而产生了多样化。所有宇宙的形态均在伟大的思想中孕育，而人们熟悉的三维空间的物质宇宙仅成为一种结果或投影。

题　记

人生一世，草木一秋。有的人一辈子执着地敲打一枚钉子，使劲地敲，直到它最后钻得很深很透。纽约州的一位普通地方法官，用自己的一生向我们诠释了完美的投资生活和他的钉子精神。在他漫长的律师职业生涯中，他的财务目标从未动摇。他想养活自己、妻子和女儿。这就意味着要支付日常账单，供女儿读完大学，支付她的婚礼费用，如果她日后需要创业启动资金，还要准备给她帮助，然后是支付养老金。除此之外的剩余应该留给孙子们做教育经费。虽然法官也为自己的一些金融举措付出了代价，但他的财务目标不仅仅是金钱。时间、烦恼、个人价值观、希望、梦想，以及其他因素与金钱捆绑，开辟了一条路径，让他达到他的目标，投资一种符合自己态度的生活。法官的一言一行在向世界展示，原来能够量入为出是多么幸福，简朴的生活同样可以充满甜蜜的滋味。

A Fully Invested Life

He was worried, having read some of my columns, that I would think he had done "everything wrong." He liked using insurance as a savings vehicle. His preferred holding period was forever. He had an affinity① for stocks in his local area — just outside of Rochester, N.Y. — and he never had an original thought about investments, preferring instead to rely on the counsel of advisers who, by his own admission, he didn't care at all if he had top-rated mutual funds, didn't sweat manager changes and was pretty sure he was not sufficiently diversified.

In his later years, he would save up all of his proxy② forms, hand them to me on a visit and tell me to let him know if he needed to do anything, or to just throw them away if I didn't want to work that hard. He surely wasn't going to read them. But what he taught me over the years is that you can do everything wrong and have it all turn out right.

When the Judge — and I met him during his long career as a village justice, so that's what I always called him — died last week at the age of 82, he left behind the extraordinary financial legacy of an ordinary

---

① affinity [ə'finiti] *n.*（指异性间的）吸引力

② proxy ['prɔksi] *n.* 代理人，代理权

完美的投资生活

读过我的某些专栏以后，他担心我会认为他做的“全都错了”。他喜欢把保险作为一种储蓄工具。他喜欢将持有股永久地保持下去。他尤其青睐纽约州罗切斯特市郊的本地股票，他对投资从来没有自己的想法，而是更喜欢依赖咨询律师的忠告，据他自己承认，他根本不关心自己有没有一流的共同基金，也不强迫管理人员做出更改，非常肯定自己的投资多元化不足。

他在晚年仍然保留着所有的代理形式，在一次来访时把它们交给我，告诉我让他知道，他是否需要做些什么，如果我不想太费神，那就把它们全部扔掉。他的确不打算读这些资料。但是多年来，他教给我的却是你可能每件事都做错了，但是放在一起看却是对的。

法官上周去世了，享年 82 岁。我在他做乡村法官的漫长岁月中与他相识，所以经常这么称呼他。他身后留下了一个普通人的非凡财产，这点遗产是经常受到人们漠视的，但它可以证明，达到良好的财务状态有很多方法，单凭这一点就十分鼓舞人心。

法官是我所认识的人中最有成就、最谦虚的人之一，对他的这

man, the kind that typically goes unseen, but that is inspiring in its proof that there are many paths to a good financial life.

One of the most accomplished and yet humble people I have known, the Judge would be embarrassed by this attention, and yet I have told so many stories in speeches over the years, I feel it would be a disservice to not discuss now how the man achieved his life's financial goals.

First, a bit of background. Tom Biddle grew up in Ann Arbor, Mich., and — like a lot of ordinary guys from that era — went off to serve in the military in World War II. During his service, he survived one of the greatest naval disasters in U.S. military history, the sinking of the troop ship Leopoldville, which claimed the lives of more than 750 men on Christmas Eve 1944. Most of his friends never knew that he nearly died in the water that night; they were unaware that those medals discreetly① mounted in a back room of the house included a Purple Heart and a Bronze Star.

After graduating from the University of Michigan and Michigan law school, he started a long career as an attorney, local justice, commissioner on the New York State Parole Board, and more. Through it all, his financial goals never wavered. He wanted to provide for himself, his wife and daughter. That meant paying the day-to-day bills, putting his daughter through college, paying for her wedding, being prepared to help her if she needed a jump-start thereafter, and then paying for retirement. Anything left over beyond that would go to an education for the

① discreetly [disˈkriːtli] *adv.* 慎重地,谨慎地

种关注肯定使他感到局促不安，但多年来，我在演讲中已经讲述了太多这样的故事，如果现在不讨论他如何实现了一生的财务目标，我觉得这对他是一种伤害。

先谈一点背景。汤姆·比德尔在美国密歇根州的安阿伯市长大，像那个时代的很多普通人一样，在“二战”中参军服役。在此期间，他经历了美国军事史上最大的海军灾难之一，即利奥波德维尔舰队的沉没，这场灾难在 1944 年圣诞前夕夺走了 750 多人的生命。他的大部分朋友从来不知道，那天晚上他差点就溺水而死。他们也不知道，那些被他小心谨慎地存放在家中密室里的奖牌，包括紫心勋章和铜星勋章。

从密歇根大学和密歇根法学院毕业后，他开始了漫长的律师职业生涯，在纽约州假释委员会担任地方法官、专员等职。他的财务目标在这一过程中从未动摇。他想养活自己、妻子和女儿。这就意味着要支付日常账单，供女儿读完大学，支付她的婚礼费用，如果她日后需要创业启动资金，还要准备给她帮助，然后是支付养老金。除此之外的剩余应该留给孙子们做教育经费。但归根结底，他的潜在目标是绝不要为钱过分担忧，尤其是在退休以后。

不要误解我的意思，如果手头没有现金，法官也会焦虑不安。为了证明他能够勉强挤出四分之一的费用以备应急，只需要瞅一眼他的财务记录。他在 1951 年购买汽油的分类账单是：一整年他只有一次花了 4 美元多买了一整桶汽油，而账单上却记录着“30 美元的基金”，他在早年时每天存一美元，既为了好玩，也是一种奢侈，

grandkids. More fundamentally, however, his underlying goal was to never have a serious worry about money, especially in retirement.

Don't get me wrong, the Judge was always nervous if the cash was in the air. For proof that he could squeeze a quarter until it screamed, one need only peek at his financial records. His 1951 gasoline purchase ledger① — he spent more than $4 for an entire tank of gas just once all year — and his records of the "$30 fund," where he effectively set aside a buck every day for fun and extravagances in his early years, were proof of just how frugal he could be and how hard he worked to live within his means. He chided me for spending $3 on a pack of 20 washcloths at Wal-Mart, noting that I probably could have gotten away for half of the towels at two-thirds of the cost. I was spending my own cash, mind you, but he didn't want it wasted.

He used insurance as a savings tool because it guaranteed that he would save, and he always worried that he might not set enough aside otherwise. He hired advisers because he wanted to focus on his law career, and he didn't enjoy investing enough to want to spend much time on it. His strategies may have "left money on the table," but he and his family never wanted for anything. Moreover, he never woke up in the middle of the night wondering if his money was safe, if he had somehow jeopardized② everything he had worked for, or if his ultimate goals were in jeopardy.

The Judge acknowledged that he "could have done some things

---

① ledger [ˈledʒə] *n.* 分类账,分户账

② jeopardize [ˈdʒepədaiz] 使濒于危险境地,冒……的危险

但却证明他是多么俭朴、多么努力地工作以设法过着量入为出的日子。他曾指责我花3美元在沃尔玛买了20条一包的浴巾，还说也许我只需用三分之二的费用，买一半数量的毛巾即可。我在用我自己的钱，关你的事吗，但他就是不想浪费钱。

他用保险作为储蓄工具，因为它保证他可以存钱，但他也总是担心，没有保险，他可能存不了足够多的钱。他聘请顾问是因为他要集中精力做好律师的工作，他不希望为了享受投资而在这上面花太多的时间。他的策略可能是“把钱放在桌子上”，但他和他的家人从来没想过要什么。此外，他也从来没有在半夜醒来，担心他的钱是否安全，担心他所做的一切是否危险，担心他的最终目标是否处于危险之中。

法官承认，他“可以把有些事做得更好”，特别是在过去的5年中，他遭受了中风的打击，身体一直衰弱，他本应该更多地关注自己的投资，即使他宁愿少点麻烦。他为自己的一些金融举措付出了代价。在他从未出售的股票中，有一支是国家城市公司的股票，这是他从母亲那儿继承来的，在过去的12个月中，这只股票急剧下跌，并已造成大量损失。谢天谢地，他从不需要依赖这笔钱。虽然他本可以带着更多的钱进坟墓，但世间令他担忧的事又少了一件，这真是个微不足道的代价。

太多的人对每一件商品、每一次交易产生的最佳结果感到担忧。他们采取行动，是因为他们认为这样做是“正确的事”。法官在当时也知道他采取了“错误”的行动，但如果结果对他来说如此

better," particularly in the past five years, since he had suffered a debilitating[①] stroke, but then he would have had to pay more attention when he preferred to pay less. He paid a price for some of his financial moves; one of those stocks he never sold was National City Corp., which he inherited from his mother and where a crushing decline in the last 12 months has resulted in a massive loss. Thankfully, he never needed to rely on that money; so while he could have gone to his grave with more, it was a small price to pay for having one less thing to worry about.

Too many people worry about getting optimal results from each and every purchase and transaction. They make moves because they feel it's the "right thing" to do. The Judge, meanwhile, knew he was making the "wrong" moves, but if they turned out so well for him, there's a real question on just how bad they could actually be. The moral of his financial story is a simple one: Financial goals are about more than just money. Factor in the time, worry, personal values, hopes, dreams, and anything else tied to money, then take a path that allows you to reach your goals, not just by the number but in keeping with your personal attitude.

The Judge got to the end of his life having accomplished everything he hoped for financially. It may not have been perfect, but it was right. We should all be so lucky.

(1,023 words)

---

① debilitating[diˈbiliteitiŋ] *adj.* 使衰弱的

之好，真正的问题只不过是它们实际上本来是多么的糟糕。从道德角度看，法官的财经故事很简单：财务目标不仅仅是金钱。时间、烦恼、个人价值观、希望、梦想以及其他与金钱捆绑的因素开辟了一条路径，让你达到你的目标，此时起作用的不仅是金钱的数量，还取决于你个人的态度。

法官走完了他的一生，完成了他在财务上所希望做的一切。也许还不够完美，但它是正确的。我们都应该这么幸运。

知识链接

Purple Heart 紫心勋章是美国发给普通士兵的第一种勋章，也是世界上颁发历史最长的一种勋章，由美国开国总统乔治·华盛顿所创立。美国士兵在执行军事任务期间只要受伤或阵亡，无论有无战功都会获得紫心勋章。

题　记

随着时代的发展和人类财富的积聚，新的财富定义也随之惹人注目地走进了大众的视线。即使房地产暴跌和全球信贷危机引发了市场翻天覆地的骤变，千万富翁在全球的各个角落和各行各业仍然保持着每年增长的势头，而超过3 000万美元的财富也只能承担它所能承担的生活水平。“现有富裕派”与“新晋富裕派”在认知价值观上的差异进一步拉大。现有富裕派宁愿付更多的佣金维持财富，教育孩子承担财政责任和慈善施舍；而新晋富裕派的观念则更多地受到消费的驱动。人们不再像“迷惘的一代”那样对金钱盲目追求，但拥有财富不一定就幸福、幸福的人一定需要拥有足够生活的财富并根植于人心的财富价值观。创造财富而不是守住财富鼓励人们游戏于投资和理财领域，引领人们对财富定义的认识进一步深化和拓展，把握住赚取财富的大好时机。

Redefining the Wealth

Even with all the upheavals① from the real estate slump and global credit crunch②, the millionaires, club has more than ten million members, and, van der Linde believes, is likely to keep growing at around 8 percent a year. The number of individuals worldwide with more than $ 1 million in investable assets grew 6 percent; this group commands more than $ 40. 7 trillion. About a third of that amount is in the hands of what Capgemini calls ultra-high-net-worth individuals, those with $ 30 million or more.

what makes the very, very rich different from the merely rich? While $ 10 million may sound like a lot of money, it's not all that much if you have children and grandchildren you want to educate and help buy homes for, says van der Linde. "You're not necessarily living a large lifestyle at that level." Above $ 30 million, however, wealth takes on a life of its own. Even at lower levels, she says, "It magnifies personality traits and

---

① upheaval[ʌpˈhiːvəl] *n.* 突然的巨变,大动荡

② crunch[krʌntʃ] *n.* 需要做出重要决策的困难时刻

重新定义财富

即使房地产暴跌和全球信贷危机引发了市场翻天覆地的骤变，但范·德·林德认为，富豪俱乐部仍有千万美元以上的富翁，并可能保持每年8%左右的增长势头。全球投资领域资产超过百万美元的人数增长了6%，这一群体掌握着40.7万亿美元以上的财富。这些财富的三分之一掌握在被凯捷咨询称为超高净值人士的手中，他们拥有3 000万美元以上的财富。

那么，非常非常富有的人士和一般的富人有什么区别呢？范·德·林德认为，尽管1 000万美元听起来很多，但如果你需要供孩子和孙子上学并帮他们买房子，那么钱就不是很多。"你没有必要过很奢侈的生活。"而超过3 000万美元的财富只能承担它所能承担的生活水平。她说，即使是较低的生活水平，"它也会放大人格特征，释放强烈的慈善热情和令人难以置信的责任感。它改变了家庭和个体之间的关系，但并非总朝着更好的方向发展"。范·德·林德回想起她所遇到的拥有不同财富的各社会阶层的富豪。"与我们合作过

brings out everything from intense philanthropic urges to an unbelievable sense of entitlement. It transforms family and personal relationships, not always for the better." Van der Linde recalls encountering social stratification among the wealthy. "A financial institution we worked with was providing seminars to the children of wealthy clients, to educate them on dealing with wealth and the responsibilities that come along with it. I was surprised to see that, when the entry-point level of wealth was lowered from $ 30 million to $ 10 million, some families at higher levels wanted to back out of the program." The reason, says van der Linde, was a difference in perceived values between "new money" and "established money." "Those with established money tend to lay more of a premium on maintaining the wealth, teaching their children about fiscal responsibility, and philanthropic① giving," she says. "The perception was that new wealth tended to be more driven by spending."

Where is all this wealth coming from? Overwhelmingly, the wealthy make their money themselves rather than inheriting it. The majority of wealth is sourced from income, and business ownership or sale of a business. Hedge fund managers, CEOs with lavish compensation packages, and successful entrepreneurs all fall into this group — and a growing proportion of them are women. "While an older generation of women may have inherited, younger women tend to be creating significant wealth in their own right."

---

① philanthropic[filən'θrɔpik] *adj.* 博爱的,慈善的

的一个金融机构承办了富豪客户研习班，教他们的孩子处理财富与随之而来的责任之间的关系。我惊讶地发现，当起点财富从3 000万美元下降到1 000万美元时，处于较高财富水平的参与家庭就会退出咨询。”范·德·林德认为，原因是“新晋富裕派”与“现有富裕派”在认知价值观上存在差异。她声称：“现有富裕派宁愿付更多的佣金维持财富，教育孩子承担财政责任和慈善施舍；而新晋富裕派的观念则更多地受到消费的驱动。”

所有这一切财富来自哪里？绝大多数富人都是自己赚钱，而不是继承遗产。大多数财富源自收入、企业产权或销售业务。对冲基金经理、拥有奢华薪酬的首席执行官以及成功的企业家都属于这个阶层，而且妇女在其中所占的比例越来越大。“虽然年龄较大的妇女有可能继承遗产，但较年轻女士往往运用自己的权利去创造巨额财富。”

财富能够带来幸福吗？它能带来幸福，对那些发现梦想或想象力已经超越金钱的人来说，尤其如此。范·德·林德说：“我遇到过几个人，他们说‘我的财富让我成为了教师，或艺术家、或音乐家，或经营基金会——如果我要倾尽全力养家糊口，就不可能有财力做其他事了。’但是，富人有富人的烦恼。他们的选择不受钱的限制，但是无论他们做什么，都会遭到周围的每一个人质疑。那些

Does wealth bring happiness? It can, especially for people who find a dream or vision that stretches beyond the money. "I'veencountered several people who say, 'My wealth allows me to be a teacher — or an artist, or a musician, or to run a foundation — something that otherwise would not have been financially possible if I had to focus on providing for my family., But," van der Linde says, "the wealthy have a different kind of struggle. Their options aren't limited by money, but everyone around them will always question whatever they do. Those who cope best are those who don't think of wealth in terms of conspicuous consumption."

Still, the rich are the most conspicuous consumers, aren't they? Not always, says van der Linde. "Someone came in to talk to us for one of our surveys. We knew his family had close to $ 100 million, but you wouldn't have given him a second look on the street. He had patches on — and holes in — his sweater. On another occasion, I kept hearing people talk about an upcoming event at a family's house. It turns out that these people had a $ 100 million art collection — and I had never heard of them, even though I then worked for a private bank dedicated to attracting precisely this type of family as clients". "People of large wealth are not always the names we read about in the newspapers. Many wealthy families tend to fly under the radar, and support the arts, for example, in a quiet fashion. Sometimes," she concludes, "the more money you have, the smaller the new cars are — but the larger the philanthropic gifts become."

应付自如的人是那些不按炫耀性消费衡量财富的人。”

不过，富人是最惹人注目的消费者，难道不是吗？范·德·林德认为，并不总是这样。“在我们的调查中，有个人来找我们谈话。我们了解到，他家有近1亿美元，但在大街上，你都不会看他第二眼。他的毛线衫上有补丁和洞。还有一次，我一直听到人们谈论即将在一个家庭的房子里举办的活动。原来这些人有1亿美元的艺术收藏品，但我从未听说过他们，虽然当时我在一家私人银行工作，而这种类型的家庭正是银行致力于吸引的客户。”她断言：“拥有巨额财富的人并不是我们经常在报纸上读到的那些名字。很多富裕的家庭宁愿保持低调，例如，用一种平淡的方式来支持艺术。有时候，你越有钱，新车就会越小，但是对慈善事业的贡献就会越大。”

人们什么时候才会觉得富有？“数量”是多少？范·德·林德说：“我认识一些人，他们觉得1 000万美元不算多。另一些人认为，达到3 000万美元才行。我认识的一个人说，他挣到2 500万美元时才会结婚，才有成就感。”根据《世界财富报告》，现在，百万富翁的平均投资资产已超过400万美元，还不包括他们的住宅价值。但是，他们感觉富裕的基准点比以往可能更高了，或者更低了。3 000万身家的女性没有富足感，因为她们没有足够的钱去做

When do people feel rich? What's "the number"? "I know people for whom $ 10 million isn't enough. Others will say they haven't made it until they hit $ 30 million. One man I know said he couldn't get married and feel successful until he had made $ 25 million." According to the World Wealth Report, the average millionaire now has more than $ 4 million in investable assets, excluding the value of their primary home. But, the point at which they feel well off can be far higher — or lower — than that. Women with $ 30 million who don't feel wealthy because they don't have the money to accomplish what they want philanthropically."

Becoming rich is one thing — how about staying rich? The first generation — the people who create wealth — tend to have survival skills and acquire a good financial education as they gradually grow their wealth. They took an active role in running their business; now they take an active role in managing their finances. They tend not to be afraid of investing, even in tough times, because their experience has shown them that this is when they find the biggest upside. It's harder for the next generation, either because they haven't had the right preparation or because they don't view the wealth as a product of what they do for a living. A woman became executor of her father's estate. She is so afraid of making the wrong move that she is paralyzed①. She has put all the money in Treasury bills.

As for building your own wealth — any strategies? Attending a

---

① paralyze[ˈpærəlaiz] *vt.*使瘫痪[麻痹]

她们想做的慈善。

致富是一回事，怎样保持富有呢？ 创造财富的第一代人随着财富的逐渐增加来获得生存技巧和良好的财务教育，他们在经营企业的过程中发挥了积极的作用。现在他们开始在管理财富方面发挥积极的作用。他们不害怕投资，甚至在经济形势不好时，他们的经验也可以告诉他们，哪些是最有价值的投资。 对第二代人来说，保住财富就有些困难，要么是因为他们还没有做好正确的准备，要么是因为他们不把财富作为他们以此为生的商品。一位女士成为她父亲财产的执行人，她非常害怕做出错误的举动，不敢做任何决策。 她把所有的钱都换成了短期国库券。

如何构建你自己的财富，有什么策略吗？ 范·德·林德在几年前参加了一个会议，令她感到震惊的是，一名演讲者引用的研究表明，所有的女性中，有84%的人最终由于丧偶、离婚、未婚等原因而独自生活。 这使她成为一名更加积极的投资者。 现在仍是单身的林德说：“我找到一个让我感到满意的顾问，告诉她我想增加自己的财富，而不是像我多年来一直在做的那样，在投资市场蜻蜓点水。”她发现石油、天然气、农产品或日用品基金等商品投资是一种获利的策略。“我看到了新兴市场的增长，认为它会需要这些产品来保持基础设施的增长。 我还注意到了消费者的行为，并开始寻找投

conference a few years ago, van der Linde was shocked to hear a speaker cite a study showing that 84 percent of all women will end their lives on their own — widowed, divorced, or unmarried. This helped make her a more proactive① investor. "I found an adviser I felt comfortable with and told her that I wanted to increase my own wealth and not just dabble② in the market the way I had been doing for years," says van der Linde, who is single. She has found that commodity investing — oil, gas, agricultural commodities, or commodities funds — has been a winning strategy. "I saw the growth in emerging markets and concluded that they would need a lot of these commodities to keep growing their infrastructure. I also pay attention to consumer behavior and look for investment ideas." Her new interests? Alternative energy and "green" businesses, where billionaires like Richard Branson are investing big bucks and venture capitalists are trying to create a new generation of fortunes for entrepreneurs. "Maybe that is what will help me grow my wealth and move me down the path toward fulfillment," she says hopefully.

(1,127 words)

---

① proactive[prəu'æktiv] *adj.*积极主动的

② dabble['dæbl] *vt.* 涉猎,浅尝

资项目。”她的新兴趣是什么？ 那就是替代能源和“绿色”企业，这也是亿万富翁理查德·布兰森投入大笔资金的领域，以及风险资本家正在试图为企业家们创造新一代财富的领域。 她满怀希望地说：“也许它可以帮我增加财富，并让我沿着这条路走下去，直到取得成功。”

知识链接

Capgemini 凯捷是全球前三大的咨询公司，也是欧洲最大的咨询公司。主要业务涵盖管理咨询、技术咨询和服务外包，主要服务领域包括能源、金融、化工、制造等。

题　记

比特币的面世开始对银行业全球支付业务的统治地位构成真正的威胁，这一互联网时代网络支付的新宠颠覆了传统的支付方式，置人们的财富价值观在虚拟与现实之间转换：尽管信用卡在在线支付市场上占主导地位，但他们的高处理成本和风险限制了其使用的范围；而比特币利用分布式数据库记录货币的交易，并使用密码学的设计确保货币流通各个环节的安全性。比特币掀起了一场全球性的货币革命，它有助于在全球实现低成本的点对点交易，而繁冗复杂的国际支付系统中善于寻租的中介机构将被淘汰。这就是比特币诡诈的魅力，它可能不是这项技术最好的驱动程序，但比特币创造的财富价值却无论如何也不可被忽视。比特币近期遇到的问题使那些吹毛求疵的人兴高采烈，比特币交易所破产的消息使成千上万客户的美元悄然流失，全球黑客攻击和与毒品有关的逮捕活动让公众对比特币讳莫如深。但实际上，比特币发动的货币革命才刚刚开始。

The Fortune Value of the Bitcoin

JPMorgan is one financial institution that has seemingly attempted to take advantage of the digital craze. The US bank recently filed for a patent for an online payment system — though it was ultimately rejected — that had a strong whiff of Bitcoin about it. JPMorgan has since dismissed the idea that its patent application was in any way inspired by Bitcoin, saying that its original patent application was made 13 years ago, before Bitcoin even took off.

That JPMorgan filed for a patent at all does nevertheless signify how serious big banks are about the evolution of online payment systems, an importance no doubt enhanced by customer demand and the meteoric, if speculative, rise of Bitcoin. The emergence of Bitcoin lit a fire under JPMorgan and pushed it to do the things its customers have been calling for it to do for years. "The big revolution we are witnessing is the emergence of the Internet for value," says Chris Larsen, CEO of Ripple Labs, the creator of the Ripple payments network, which is online and global. "The world has learned how to build value exchange systems without a central operator." He adds that JPMorgan's patent suggests that

比特币的财富价值

摩根大通是一个似乎试图利用数码新潮流的金融机构。这家美国银行最近申请了一个在线支付系统的专利，虽然这项专利最终遭到了拒绝，但它充斥着浓烈的比特币味道。摩根大通后来驳回了其专利申请是在某种程度上受比特币启发的主意，声称最初的专利申请是在 13 年前，那时比特币还没有火爆起来。

然而，在任何情况下，摩根大通申请专利都意味着大银行在在线支付系统发展过程中的严肃态度。如果冒险一些说，客户需求和比特币的快速崛起无疑增强了其重要性。比特币的出现在摩根大通点了一把火，推动其开展客户多年来一直呼吁的事情。Ripple Labs 的首席执行官、在线和全球支付网络 Ripple 的创建者克里斯·拉尔森认为："我们正在见证的大革命是互联网价值的出现，世界已经学会如何在没有中央操作系统时构建价值交换系统。"他补充说，摩根大通的专利证实了它正在设计适合互联网时代的自己的支付系统。

事实上，摩根大通的专利申请表明，尽管信用卡在在线支付市场上占主导地位，并可能持续至少 5 年，但他们的高处理成本和风

it is now under way in designing its own payments system suited to the Internet age.

Indeed, JPMorgan's patent application said that although credit cards dominate the market for online payments — and are likely to continue to do so for at least five years — their high processing costs and risks limit their use. The bank says what the Internet needs is something that is a quick, cheap and simple way of transferring value. What they propose is a means of making anonymous payments "without provision of an account number or name from the payer". Their system would make Internet shopping safer by withholding information from merchants that allow them to withdraw money from customer accounts, the demand for which has existed for years.

This is bit-bucks or bitcoin. You can call them e-backs, if you like, or digital dollars. Despite the triumphalism① of bitcoin's naysayers at the present, crypto-currencies aren't doomed. You can't suppress an innovation that permits global, low-cost peer-to-peer transactions and which renders obsolete the rent-seeking intermediaries of a cumbersome international payments system. It's just that for all bitcoin's quirky② charms, it might not be the best driver for this technology, however, the fortune Value created by the Bitcoin could not in any way be neglected.

So, where does this process go?

---

① triumphalism [traiˈʌmf(ə)liz(ə)m] *n.* 必胜信念,必胜心态

② quirky [ˈkwɜːki] *adj.* 古怪的,离奇的

险限制了其使用的范围。银行方面表示，互联网所需要的是一个快捷、廉价和简单的方式来转移价值。他们打算用一种匿名支付的方法，“不提供付款人的账户号码或姓名”。他们的系统对商家隐瞒信息，以防止商人从消费者的账户里面取钱，这样可以使网购更加安全，这种需求已经存在很多年了。

这就是比特美元，或比特币。你可以叫他们电子美元，当然如果你喜欢，也可以称之为数字美元。尽管比特币的反对者现阶段大获全胜，但虚拟货币并没有被判死刑。你不可能抑制一场全球性的货币革命，它有助于在全球实现低成本的点对点交易，而繁冗复杂的国际支付系统中善于寻租的中介机构将被淘汰。这就是比特币诡诈的魅力，它可能不是这项技术最好的驱动程序，但比特币创造的财富价值却无论如何也不可被忽视。

那么，这将是一个怎样的过程呢?

虽然目前距离实现上述目标还很遥远，但比特币的最终游戏规则是将法定货币数字化，即比特币誓要颠覆由政府支持的那些摇摇欲坠的纸币形式。如果是这样的话，我们还是要做好迎接新的世界秩序的准备。数字美元会让热衷于虚拟货币的人感到不安，他们认为，由私营部门开发的数字货币尽管能摆脱纸币诅咒，但它的支撑者毕竟不是政府而是达成网络共识的计算机业主。他们警告说，恣意妄为的政客和自私自利的银行人士习惯让本国货币贬值，让公众为通货膨胀买单，使人们丧失购买力以及对政府的信任。

It's a ways off, but the end game could be the digitalization of fiat currencies, those creaky government-backed forms of paper money that bitcoin vows to disrupt. If so, get ready for a new world order. A digital dollar would alarm crypto-currency enthusiasts who see privately developed digital currencies — backed not by a government but by consensus-building networks of computer owners — as an escape from the curse of paper currencies. They warn that profligate① politicians and self-interested bankers habitually debase national currencies and lump citizens with the bill by way of inflation, lost purchasing power and unaccountable government.

However, Average Joes are now also looking warily at these techies' newfangled alternatives — evident in the comments stream on stories about the collapse of bitcoin exchange Mt. Gox. Ordinary folk have been burned by both Washington and Wall Street, but at least they understand those animals, or think they do. How are they to trust a complicated collection of bits and bytes that's "mined" by a network of anonymous computers and exploited by geeks via offshore, unregulated and highly unstable exchanges? Above all, money is about trust.

Still, mind-blowing new digital-currency ideas seem to arrive daily, bitcoin-based sales are growing steadily, and serious institutional investors are unveiling plans for large-scale, regulated exchanges. Financial innovation is unstoppable, which means society is headed for a

① profligate [ˈprɔfligət] *adj.* 恣意挥霍的

不过，普通人目前也还在警惕地观望这些技术人员发布的新流行的替代货币，这从比特币交易所 Mt. Gox 倒闭事件引发的一系列评论中就可以看出。普通民众已经对华盛顿和华尔街极度愤怒，但是他们至少还能理解、或自以为理解这些“禽兽”。如何让普通民众相信一个由匿名的计算机用户构建的网络“挖矿”、并由极客们通过离岸开发所得的复杂代码组成的虚拟货币？况且虚拟货币还没有得到监管，交易也不稳定。毕竟，货币需要的是信任。

不过，令人兴奋的新的数字货币理念似乎已经进入到我们的日常生活，以比特币为基础的交易稳步增长，严肃认真的机构投资者正在赤裸裸地计划建设大规模、受监管的交易所。金融创新是不可阻挡的，这意味着社会正在走向一个关键点。它将推动创新者参与竞争，利用手中的技术，承诺削减成本和整合数十亿人类，使他们进入一个更有效的全球金融体系。不可避免的是，政府将通过谈判获得一份妥协方案。而这可能是因为他们实际上加入了虚拟货币革命。

加拿大已经在对加拿大元进行所谓的 MintChip 数字货币实验。但真正能改变世界货币格局的应该是数字美元。康奈尔大学教授、前国际货币基金组织的经济学家埃斯瓦尔·普拉萨德认为，如果建立了根深蒂固的数字美元，“国家边界将不再有太大的意义。”如果公民能够通过点击鼠标获得世界上最抢手货币的数字版本的美元，中国、俄罗斯和阿根廷等国将很难以通过资本管制将本国的金融体

showdown. It will pit the innovators, armed with a technology that promises to slash costs and integrate billions of human beings into a more efficient global financial system. Inevitably, governments will negotiate a compromise. And it could be that they actually join the crypto-currency revolution.

Canada is already experimenting with a digital version of its dollar, the so-called MintChip. But the real game-changer would be a digital U.S. dollar. And if that becomes entrenched, "national borders are not going to have much meaning anymore," says Cornell professor and former IMF economist Eswar Prasad. If their citizens can obtain and use a digital version of the world's most sought-after currency by clicking a mouse, countries like China, Russia and Argentina will find it harder to insulate their financial systems with capital controls. They'd try to censor the Internet or ban access to foreign currency, but the digital dollar would eventually seep in to supplant the yuan, ruble or peso for internal and external commerce.

"The walls that countries try to put up around capital inflows and outflows, those are going to disappear very, very quickly," said Mr. Prasad, whose new book, "The Dollar Trap," explains how the greenback came to dominate the global economy. And that's not all. Central banks could use digital fiat currencies to get around the "zero-bound" problem that forced them into massive money-printing programs once they'd cut interest rates to zero after the 2008 financial crisis. If digital currencies were to fully replace their paper equivalents, central

系与外界隔离。这些国家会试图审查互联网或禁止外币的入口，但数字美元会最终渗透进来，在这些国家的境内外商业活动中取代人民币、卢布和比索。

普拉萨德先生的新书《美元陷阱》解释了美元如何成为主宰全球经济的货币。他说："各国控制资本流入和流出的铜墙铁壁，将消失得非常非常快。"不仅如此。央行可以利用数字法定货币绕过"零利率"问题，在2008年金融危机之后，一旦他们将利率下调至零，这个问题就迫使他们进入大规模的印钞时代。如果数字货币能完全取代纸币，央行就可以对银行账户征税，因为储户无法通过储存现金来逃税，实际上等同于设定了负利率。

当然，一想到那个无所不能、大张旗鼓地削减你的储蓄的央行，那些鼓吹比特币独立性的人就会感到心惊胆战。但它无疑要好过无尽的"量化宽松"政策，它使金融家赚得盆满钵满，但却未能给数以百万计的人创造就业机会。眼下，低于通货膨胀的利率已经侵蚀了美元的消费能力。不过，虽然这实际上等同于有名无实地减少了用户储蓄，家庭和企业通常不会认为是等价的资产损失，这使得央行更难以激励消费，刺激经济和创造就业机会。整个社会的通货膨胀分布并不均衡。负利率将是一个更公平、更有效的工具。那么，对自由使用比特币者的好消息是：有可能创建私有的数字货币来替代法定货币。在未来，联邦储备系统不是由被银行游说者资助的国会议员来承担责任，而是受任何人都可以发起竞争性货币的

banks could tax bank accounts — effectively setting a negative rate — since depositors could no longer flee the taxman by storing dollars under the mattress.

For sure, the idea of an all-powerful central bank literally cutting your savings is horrendous for those who trumpet bitcoin's independence. But it is arguably preferable to endless "quantitative easing" programs, which have lined the pockets of financiers but failed to create jobs for tens of millions. Right now, interest rates below inflation are already eroding the dollar's spending power. But although that's effectively the same as nominally reducing savings, households and businesses typically don't perceive the same loss of value, making it harder for central banks to incentivize spending, stimulate the economy and create jobs. And inflation is unevenly distributed across society. Negative interest rates would be a fairer and more effective tool. Well, the good news for libertarian bitcoiners is that it's possible to create private, digital alternatives to fiat currencies. In the future, the Fed won't be held to account by bank lobbyist-funded Congressmen but by a global marketplace in which anyone can issue a competing currency.

Bitcoin's recent problems have enlivened its critics. News of bankrupt exchanges losing hundreds of millions of customers, dollars, worldwide hacking attacks and drug-related arrests can do that to the public. But in fact, the revolution it unleashed is only just beginning.

(1,107 words)

全球市场的支配。

比特币近期遇到的问题使那些吹毛求疵的人兴高采烈。比特币交易所破产的消息使成千上万客户的美元悄然流失，全球黑客攻击和与毒品有关的逮捕活动让公众对比特币讳莫如深。但实际上，比特币发动的货币革命才刚刚开始。

知识链接

Bitcoin 比特币。比特币最初由中本聪在 2009 年提出，并根据中本聪的思路设计发布了开源软件以及建构其上的 P2P 网络。比特币是一种 P2P 形式的数字货币。与大多数货币不同，比特币不依靠特定货币机构发行，它依据特定算法，通过大量的计算产生，比特币经济使用整个 P2P 网络中众多节点构成的分布式数据库来确认并记录所有的交易行为，并使用密码学的设计来确保货币流通各个环节的安全性。比特币可以用来兑现，可以兑换成大多数国家的货币。使用者可以用比特币购买一些虚拟物品，比如网络游戏当中的衣服、帽子、装备等，只要有人接受，也可以使用比特币购买现实生活当中的物品。

Mt. Gox 位于日本东京的 Mt. Gox（昵称：门头沟）是世界上最大的比特币交易商，承担着超过 80% 的比特币交易。不幸的是，Mt. Gox 发生了被盗事件，丢失了 85 万枚比特币，按市价约为 5 亿美元，于 2014 年 2 月 28 日申请了破产保护。

题　记

作者辞去一家全球共同基金副主席的职务，创办了一份投资简讯，在帮助他人稳妥地赚钱的同时充满激情地做着自己最喜欢的事业。这就是真实财富投资成功的最大秘诀。发现和创造你人生的工作机会，会给你带来更多的财富，实现你的人生价值，因为财富的原则就是在快乐中获取，在快乐中消费。作者的创业是一段从游泳池边开始的漫长行程，与之异曲同工的还有从大学宿舍楼走出的戴尔电脑、从车库里研制出的苹果系列产品、诞生于地下室的智必星品牌、在哈佛校园链接全球的脸书网……创造财富需要勇气和胆量，寻找财富则需要智慧和机缘，而管理财富更是一门学问。如果你面对财富的机会能够长袖善舞，那么你将花人生最少的能量取得最大的快乐与幸福。

The Secret to True Wealth Investing

Eleven years ago, I quit my job as the vice president of a global mutual fund, and I decided I wanted to write an investment newsletter.

Right out of college, I was a broker for a year or two at a firm specializing in global stocks and bonds. One thing that struck me was that most of my clients were readers of investment newsletters, Mark Skousen's, Adrian Day's, and the Oxford Club, among others. That firm also ran a small ($ 50 million) fund and, at 24 years old, I became vice president. Running a global mutual fund was my dream job at the time. Unfortunately, the company knew it. So it paid me a tiny annual salary of $ 23,500! It was a big pay cut.

But I would have been stupid not to take that job. The fund was small, so I wore every hat at times, research, trading, bookkeeping, SEC compliance, accounting, writing the quarterly reports, it was a great experience. After a year, though, when they offered me a small raise to $ 27,000, I would have been stupid to stay. I'd started studying for a Ph.D. while working for the fund. Between tuition and rent, my net

真实财富的投资秘诀

11 年前，我辞去了一家全球共同基金副主席的职务，打算创办一份投资简讯。

大学一毕业，我在一家专营全球股票和债券的公司做了一两年的经纪人。有一件事给我留下了深刻的印象，那就是我的大多数客户都是投资简讯的读者，其中包括马克·斯考森年代、艾德里安·敦伊年代以及牛津俱乐部等。这家公司也经营5 000万美元的小额基金，我 24 岁时晋升为公司的副主席。那时，经营全球共有基金是我梦寐以求的工作。不幸的是，公司知道了我的想法，因此仅仅给我 2.35 万美元的年薪。这个报酬压得太低了。

但是，如果不接受这份工作我就更蠢。这家共有基金规模很小，因此我可以不时地尝试各种职位，包括研究、贸易、簿记、证交会规定、会计、写季度报告等，这是一种很棒的经历。一年之后，公司将我的年薪小幅调升至 2.7 万美元，我留下来真是愚蠢。我边为公司工作边开始攻读博士学位。受学费和住房租金的夹击，我的收入净值一天天减少。

于是，我辞职了。我清楚地记得，我去了女朋友的公寓大楼，

worth was shrinking every day.

So I quit. I distinctly remember going over to my girlfriend's apartment complex and telling her what I'd just done. And then on the pool deck, I laid out a half dozen investment newsletters. I told her, this is what I want to do. "I can do better than these, I think." I told her. "What do you mean, better?" she asked. I didn't really know. "Can you make money doing this?" I didn't really know. "Well, how do you get readers?" Once again, I didn't really know. It wasn't a thought-out plan. I just thought that I could help a lot of people do a lot better with their own money.

My former boss at the brokerage firm was kind enough to get in touch with Julia Guth of the Oxford Club newsletter for me. And in just a few weeks, I moved and was writing a newsletter. Two years later, I was writing the Oxford Club letter with 45,000 readers — a long way from the pool deck!

The dream had come true. I was helping investors. Even better, the girlfriend with the good questions by the pool became my wife. I'll turn 36 next year, and we have two little kids, ages five and three. We are so thankful for how things have worked out.

My childhood friend Porter Stanberry talked to me about starting my own letter, True Wealth, about writing whatever I wanted. He even offered a "blank check" and research budget. I couldn't refuse that! But I knew that I would be a hard to sell to readers. they'vealways said I'm too conservative an investor for the newsletter business. Another thing that

并告诉她我所做的事情。然后，在游泳池边，我编排了半打的投资简讯。我告诉她，这就是我想做的事。我对她说，“我认为，我可以做得比这更好”。她问我，“你的更好是什么意思？”我真的不知道。她问我，“发行刊物能挣钱吗？”我真的不知道。“你怎样吸引读者？”我再次表示真的不知道。这不是一个深思熟虑的计划。我只是想，我能帮助很多人更好地理财。

我在经纪公司的前任老板非常热心地帮我联系上了牛津俱乐部投资简讯的朱莉娅·古斯。几个星期后，我开始行动，并出版了一份简讯。两年后，我开始给牛津俱乐部写简讯，读者人数达 4.5 万。这真是一段从游泳池边开始的漫长行程。

我的梦想已经实现了。我正在帮助投资者。更让我开心的是，在游泳池边向我提出那些好问题的女朋友成了我的妻子。明年我就 36 岁了，我们有两个小孩，一个 5 岁，一个 3 岁。我们非常庆幸，事情进展得如此顺利。

这时，我儿时的伙伴波特·斯坦勃利找我商讨，能否创办我自己的刊物，名为《真实财富》，我想写什么就写什么。他甚至给我提供了一张“空白支票”和研究预算。我不可能拒绝它！但我知道，刊物很难卖给读者。他们总是认为，就投资生意而言，我是一名太过保守的投资者。我从不购买投资领域里的流行产品，这是销售艰难的另一个原因。

很显然，做不受欢迎的事似乎也还行。尽管有很大的分歧，但是我们成功了。《真实财富》成为国内最大的投资资讯之一。对于

makes the sale hard is that I never buy what's popular in the investment world.

Apparently, doing what's unpopular seems to work. Against great odds, we made it. True Wealth has become one of the largest investment newsletters in the country. For a conservative letter with no hot "hook," that's an achievement, but I'm just thankful to be doing what I love to do. With this month being the fifth anniversary of my first True Wealth issue, I decided to kick off my presentation at last week's Alliance Conference with my five best investment recommendations right now.

Out of fairness to my paid subscribers, I can't mention my two newest (and most hated by the public) investment ideas. I can tell you, however, the three investments for the long run that I'verecently mentioned in the pages of Daily Wealth: Icelandic bonds, collectibles, and Japanese real estate.

I can't possibly be an expert in all of these different things, of course. I do my best to find things that fit into our criteria, and then I find experts to help me uncover the best ideas. For example, I don't know how many trips I'vemade to Iceland in the last few years checking things out. It's at least a half dozen. And I'vemet with the local brokerage① firms and feel extremely comfortable that our money is absolutely fine there.

Shifting gears to Japanese real estate. I think Japanese real estate will be an extraordinary investment for a very long time. Real estate nationwide

① brokerage [ˈbrəukəridʒ] *n.* 经纪人(或中间人)业务

一个保守、缺乏“吸引”热点的专刊而言，这当然是个成就，而我非常感激的是我正在做我热爱的事业。这个月是我的第一本专刊《真实财富》发行5周年纪念，我打算抛开我上周在联合会议上的演讲，及时提出五个最好的投资建议。

出于对专刊订阅者公平，我无法涉及两个最新的、也是最不受公众欢迎的投资理念。但是我可以告诉你，我最近在“每日财富”专栏中提到了三个长期投资领域：冰岛债券、募集债券和日本房地产。

当然，我不可能是所有这些不同领域的专家，但我会竭尽所能找出适合我们标准的东西，然后请专家帮我找出最好的投资理念。例如，我不知道在过去的几年中，为了核实情况，我到底去过几次冰岛，至少有6次了吧。我曾经和当地的经纪公司接洽，感觉我们的资金在那里绝对安全。

再转到日本的房地产。我认为，在相当长的时间内，日本房地产将是一个特别的投资。自20世纪90年代以来，国内房地产市场迄今一直在衰退。利率确实很低。大堆积压的储蓄没有利息，我甚至怀疑政府会阻碍房地产市场的繁荣。所以，在最近一期的“舒哥德机密”专栏中，我推荐了一支小型的日本房地产股票。我的哥哥，现任美国一家大型法律公司的律师，打算转入东京的并购工作。他正在学习日语。我希望明年去那儿考察时，他会是一位不错的当地联络员。我认为这三种投资都有潜力，未来多年都能取得非凡的投资回报率。

has fallen every year since 1990, until now. Interest rates are really low. There's a huge pile of pent-up savings earning no interest, and I seriously doubt the government will get in the way of a housing boom. So in the latest issue of Sjuggerud Confidential, I recommended a small Japanese real-estate stock. My brother, who is currently an attorney for a major law firm in the U. S., is transferring to Tokyo to work on mergers① and acquisitions. He's been studying Japanese. I'm hoping he'll be a great local contact for us next year, as I travel there to check things out. I think these three investments have the potential to make extraordinary returns for many years to come.

Even though all of these investments sound unrelated, they all share the same characteristics we look for in a buy — they're exceptional values, that are ignored, often hated, and are just beginning their uptrends. Those are the secrets to True Wealth investing.

But the biggest secret to the success of True Wealth? I think the "secret" is simply that I'm passionate about what I'm doing. And that is helping people grow their money safely.

(931 words)

---

① merger [ˈməːdʒə] v. (两个或以上公司的)合并,并吞

尽管所有这些投资听起来似乎没有联系，但我们在寻求购买时，它们都具备相同的特征，即它们是被忽视、通常不受欢迎的例外值，只是刚开始有向上的趋势。这些就是“真实财富”投资的秘诀。

然而，什么是“真实财富”投资成功的最大秘诀呢？我认为，“秘诀”很简单，即我对我正在做的事情充满激情，那就是帮助人们稳妥地赚钱。

知识链接

SEC 美国证券交易委员会（the U. S. Securities and Exchange Commission，简称 SEC）。美国证交会是美国证券行业的最高机构，根据 1934 年根据证券交易法令而成立，直属美国联邦并负责美国的证券监督和管理工作，具有准立法权、准司法权、独立执法权。

题　记

人类对于未来情感的预期，往往和实际有着很大的“预测偏差”：我们从不满足。在追求快乐的过程中，加薪、豪华跑车和彩票中奖都是我们为之奋斗的目标。可是，一旦得到了梦寐以求的东西，我们的不满之心很快就又会被其他的物质欲望撩拨得蠢蠢欲动，随后便开始新一轮的物质追逐。事实上，一旦人的基本需求得到满足，更多的钱并不能带来更多的快乐。当我们拥有更多的财富时，总是高估了从中可以得到的快乐；钱越多引发的压力越大，从高收入工作中获得的高薪也许不能买到太多的快乐；当我们读到荒诞的富人们纸醉金迷的生活时，会感到一丝嫉妒，但是我们常拿来和自己相比较的通常是平常人。“快乐购物清单”或许可以让我们放慢这种不断追求物质享受的脚步，回归普通人的幸福和快乐：浪漫、淡定和感激。

Happiness Shopping List

"Whoever said money can't buy happiness isn't spending it right." You may remember those Lexus ads from a few years ago, What made the ads so intriguing①, but also so infuriating②, was mainly that they seemed to offer a simple — if rather expensive — solution to a common question: How can you transform the money you work so hard to earn into something approaching the good life? You know that there must be some connection between money and happiness. If there weren't, you'd be less likely to stay late at work or struggle to save money and invest it profitably. But then why aren't your lucrative③ promotion and five-bedroom house cheering you up? The relationship between money and happiness, it would appear, is more complicated than the romantic entanglements④ of any Desperate Housewife.

---

① intriguing [in'triːgiŋ] *a.* 吸引人的，有趣的
② infuriating [in'fjuərieitiŋ] *a.* 令人发怒的
③ lucrative ['luːkrətiv] *a.* 有利益的，合算的
④ entanglement [in'tæŋglmənt] *n.* 纠缠，牵连

快乐购物清单

“那些说金钱买不到快乐的人没有把钱花在正确的地方。”你可能记得几年以前的凌志汽车广告，这则广告之所以如此吸引人、又使人极为不满，主要是因为他们似乎提供了一个简单而昂贵的解决方案来回答一个平常的问题：你如何用辛辛苦苦赚来的钱过上美好的生活？ 你要知道，金钱和快乐之间一定有某种联系。 如果没有，你不可能工作到很晚，或者拼命存钱和投资盈利。 但是，为什么增加薪资和五居室的房子并不能让你感到快乐呢？ 金钱和快乐的关系似乎比任何“绝望主妇”的情感纠葛更复杂。

幸运的是，你不必自己解结。 在过去的 25 年里，经济学家和心理学家们共同努力，将“如何”、“为什么”、“为什么不”进行了分类。 尤其是“为什么不”。 为什么你的钱越多，你想得到的就越多？ 为什么购买你梦想中的车、高级公寓或者手机不能给你带来更多短暂的快乐？

为了回答这些看上去令人沮丧的问题，研究快乐的新学者们深

Fortunately, you don't have to do the untangling① yourself. Over the past quarter-century, economists and psychologists have banded together to sort out the hows, whys and why nots of money and mood. Especially the why nots. Why is it that the more money you have, the more you want? Why doesn't buying the car, condo or cell phone of your dreams bring you more than momentary joy?

In attempting to answer these seemingly depressing questions, the new scholars of happiness have arrived at some insights that are downright cheery. Money can help you find more happiness, so long as you know just what you can and can't expect from it. And you don't have to buy a Lexus to be happy. Much of the research suggests that seeking the good life at a store is an expensive exercise in futility②. Before you can pursue happiness the right way, you need to recognize what you'vebeen doing wrong.

The new science of happiness starts with a simple insight: We're never satisfied. "We always think if we just had a little bit more money, we'd be happier," says Catherine Sanderson, a psychology professor at Amherst College, "but when we get there, we're not." Indeed, the more you make, the more you want. The more you have, the less effective it is at bringing you joy, and that seeming paradox has long bedeviled economists. "Once you get basic human needs met, a lot more

---

① untangle [ˌʌnˈtæŋgl] *v.* 解开纠结,排解
② futility [fjuːˈtiləti] *n.* 无用,无益

入了解了一些的确令人愉快的现象。金钱能帮助你找到更多的快乐，只要你知道你能从金钱中得到什么、不能得到什么。你没有必要购买凌志汽车以博开心。大部分研究表明，在商店里寻找美好生活是毫无意义的昂贵消费。在以正确的方式追求快乐之前，你需要认识到你一直以来做错了什么。

新的快乐科学从一个简单的考察开始：我们从不满足。阿姆赫斯特学院的心理学教授凯瑟琳·桑得森说："我们总是想，要是我们有稍多一点的钱，我们就会快乐得多。但钱到手之后，我们并不快乐。"确实，你得到的越多，你想要的就越多。你拥有的越多，它带给你的快乐就不那么有效，这看上去自相矛盾的说法一直困扰着经济学家。哈佛大学心理学教授、《遭遇幸福》一书的作者丹·吉尔伯特认为，"一旦人的基本需求得到满足，更多的钱并不能给你带来更多的快乐"。尽管富人比穷人更快乐，但过去50年来生活水平的巨大提高并没有使美国人更快乐。为什么呢？这里有三个原因：

当你拥有更多的财富时，你高估了从中可以得到的快乐。人类是适应性的动物，这在冰河时代、瘟疫和战争期间一直是个有利因素。但是，那也是你为什么在好运来到你面前时，也从不满足。虽然赚更多的钱让你在短期内获得快乐，但是你很快适应了新的财

money doesn't make a lot more happiness," notes Dan Gilbert, a psychology professor at Harvard University and the author of the book Stumbling on Happiness. And while the rich are happier than the poor, the enormous rise in living standards over the past 50 years hasn't made Americans happier. Why? Three reasons:

You overestimate how much pleasure you'll get from having more. Humans are adaptable creatures, which has been a plus during assorted ice ages, plagues and wars. But that's also why you're never all that satisfied for long when good fortune comes your way. While earning more makes you happy in the short term, you quickly adjust to your new wealth — and everything it buys you. Yes, you get a thrill at first from shiny new cars and TV screens the size of Picasso's Guernica. But you soon get used to them, a state of running in place that economists call the "hedonic treadmill①."

Even though stuff seldom brings you the satisfaction you expect, you keep returning to the mall and the car dealership in search of more. "When you imagine how much you're going to enjoy a Porsche, what you're imagining is the day you get it," says Gilbert. When your new car loses its ability to make your heart go pitter-patter, you tend to draw the wrong conclusions. Instead of questioning the notion that you can buy happiness on the car lot, you begin to question your choice of car. So you pin your hopes on a new BMW, only to be disappointed again.

---

① hedonic treadmill 享乐适应症

富——它给你带来了一切。刚得到闪亮的新车和毕加索名画格尔尼卡大小的电视屏幕时，你会感到刺激。但是你很快就习惯了，经济学家们把这种原地踏步状态称为“享乐适应征”。

即使你很少从商品中得到你期望的满足感，但你仍然流连于购物中心和汽车经销中心，以寻找更多的快乐。吉尔伯特说：“当你想象保时捷汽车能给你带来多少享受时，你想象的只是你得到它的那一天。”当新车不能让你的心脏怦怦直跳时，你很容易得出错误的结论。你质疑的不是能否从停车场买到快乐的观点，而是开始质疑自己对车的选择。于是你寄希望于新的宝马，只不过再次失望罢了。

钱越多引发的压力也越大。从高收入工作中获得的高薪也许不能买到太多的快乐。但是，它能让你买到郊外宽敞的大房子。问题是，这也意味着长距离的工作往返，反复的研究证实了你每天的感觉：即使你热爱你的工作，但是，每天那么一小段你称之为地狱般的往返行程也会让你精疲力竭。你可以适应大多数事情，但不管是上班的第一天还是最后一天，走走停停的车辆或者超载的公共汽车都会让你不开心。

你不断地和隔壁的邻居做比较。H.L.门肯就曾取笑过快乐的男人，说他比自己小姨子的老公多挣了100美元。他是对的。研究

More money can lead to more stress. The big salary you pull in from your high-paying job may not buy you much in the way of happiness. But it can buy you a spacious house in the suburbs. Trouble is, that also means a long trip to and from work, and study after study confirms what you sense daily: Even if you love your job, the little slice of everyday hell you call the commute can wear you down. You can adjust to most anything, but a stop-and-go drive or an overstuffed bus will make you unhappy whether it's your first day on the job or your last.

You endlessly compare yourself with the family next door. H. L. Mencken once quipped that the happy man was one who earned $100 more than his wife's sister's husband. He was right. Happiness scholars have found that how you stand relative to others makes a much bigger difference to your sense of well-being than how much you make in an absolute sense.

You may feel a touch of envy when you read about the glamorous lives of the absurdly wealthy, but the group you likely compare yourself with are folks Harvard economist Erzo Luttmer calls "similar others" — the people you work with, people you grew up with, old friends and old classmates. "You have to think, 'I could have been that person,'" Luttmer says.

If you want to know how to use the money you have to become happier, you need to understand just what it is that brings you happiness in the first place. And that's where the newest happiness research comes in. Read carefully the following Happiness Shopping List.

快乐的学者发现，在相对和绝对的比较中，你对幸福的感觉有很大的不同。当你读到荒诞的富人们纸醉金迷的生活时，你会感到一丝嫉妒，但是你爱拿来和你自己相比较的通常是平常人，哈佛大学经济学家埃佐·鲁特莫称之为“相似的其他人”，即和你一起工作的人，和你一起长大的人，老朋友和老同学。鲁特莫说：“你总在想‘本来我也会成为那样的人的’。”

如果你想知道如何用钱，你必须变得更快乐，你首先需要理解给你带来快乐的是什么。这就是最新的快乐研究得出的成果。请仔细阅读下面的这份“快乐购物清单”。

浪漫——打玫瑰花

你可能会笑话岳父母和老式的家庭拖累，但是，分类研究已经发现，已婚的人一般比单身更快乐。做那些能保持你婚姻快乐的事情，包括偶尔给你的爱人买一束60美元的玫瑰花。

淡定——吉他课程

快乐人士的生活需要极度的淡定，例如，掌握一门乐器、打18洞的高尔夫球或者完成纵横字谜游戏，而高度紧张感和全神贯注的状态来自需要技术和注意力高度集中的爱好。

宠物——猫或狗

尽管它们捣毁了所有的沙发和鞋子，但宠物已被证明能给人带

ROMANCE —A DOZEN ROSES

You may joke about in-laws and the old ball and chain, but an assortment of studies have found that married people are generally happier than singles. Do what you can to keep your marriage a happy one, including buying your sweetie the occasional $ 60 bouquet of roses.

FLOW — GUITAR LESSONS

The lives of happy people tend to have a lot of flow — the high-intensity, utterly absorbing state that can come from a hobby that takes skill and concentration — for example, mastering an instrument, playing 18 holes of golf or finishing a crossword puzzle.

PET — CAT OR DOG

Despite all the sofas and shoes they destroy, pets have been shown to make you happier. What's more, caring for furry friends can help ease stress.

GRATITUDE — JOURNAL

A recent study found that writing down what you're grateful for leaves you happier and more optimistic. Buy a fancy $ 30 leather journal— or a $ 1. 50 composition notebook — and take a few moments every day or week to reflect on your good life and to record it.

(1,098 words)

来更多的快乐。 另外，照顾小动物能帮你缓解压力。

感激——日记

最近的研究发现，记下你感激的事情会让你更开心和更乐观。买一个精致的30美元的皮革日记本，或者1.5美元的笔记本，每天或每星期花点时间回味你的美好生活，然后把它记下来。

知识链接

BStumbling on Happiness 《遭遇幸福》是社会心理学家、哈佛大学教授丹尼尔·吉尔伯特的著作。书中列举了大量怪诞的实验，引用了大量的心理学和行为科学方面的研究成果，证明了这样一个事实：我们都有一个与生俱来的"幸福基础值"，生活中的成就与挫折，往往只是短暂地改变我们的幸福水平。很快地，我们就会回归自己的"幸福基础值"。现代社会的人们拥有自主的选择权，我们的幸福掌握在自己手中，所以人们应当"智慧地购买"幸福，提升自己的"幸福基础值"。

题　记

《了不起的盖茨比》是“迷惘一代”的代表作家 F. 斯科特·菲茨杰拉德最成功的小说。主人公盖茨比为了赢得爱情，不择手段地聚积金钱，但是物质上的巨大成功并没有让他的理想变成现实，他带着残破的美国梦离开了这个世界。人类的天真与蛮横、光荣与梦想在爱情与财富的交织中被表现得淋漓尽致。补偿性工资差异理论重新论证了伊斯特林悖论：一份越是令人厌恶、越是危险的工作，它的报酬就越高；大的保险理赔往往付给了那些愿意做具有道德疑问工作的高素质人员。盖茨比的葬礼也再次论证了伊斯特林悖论：愿意出席葬礼的人寥寥无几，曾经的夜夜笙歌、纸醉金迷落在了城市一望无垠的昏暗之中，那些有意识地特别专注物质成功的人，可享有的衡量幸福的指数是如此令人感慨。“盖茨比”指南成为一个时代留给后来的财富追求者们最难忘的旋律之一。

"Gatsby" Guidebook

Interest in the lifestyles of the rich and famous varies with economic conditions. Just as someone who is seven feet tall may seem almost normal at an N.B.A. practice session, the purchases of the wealthy typically attract little notice when inequality is low and stable. But when inequality is high and growing rapidly, luxury purchases are sometimes as hard to ignore as a seven-foot ninth grader.

When "The Great Gatsby" was first published in 1925, income and wealth disparities① were at record levels. It is thus no mystery that F. Scott Fitzgerald's tale of wealthy Americans during the Jazz Age became an instant best seller. Inequality diminished rapidly during the Great Depression and remained low until the 1970's. But since then, it has again been rising sharply. Today, disparities are once more at record levels, which may help explain the resurgence of interest in Gatsby. Fitzgerald's novel was recently selected, for example, for common reading programs at Cornell and other universities, programs in which students, faculty members, alumni② and others on the staff are

---

① disparity [di'spæriti] *n.* 差异,不一致

② alumni [ə'lʌmnai] *n.* 男毕业生,男校友

“盖茨比”指南

对富人、名人生活方式的兴趣随经济状况的改变而改变。就像7英尺的身高在NBA很正常一样，当贫富不均幅度不大、且比较稳定的时候，富人的采购几乎不会引起什么关注。但是当贫富不均明显，并日益扩大时，奢侈品采购有时就很难被忽略，就像看见一位身高7英尺的园丁一样。

自1925年《了不起的盖茨比》首次出版以来，收入和财富不均屡破纪录。因此，F.斯科特·菲茨杰拉德所写的关于爵士乐时代富有的美国人的故事当即成为畅销书就没什么神秘可言了。贫富不均在大萧条期间迅速缩小，并且一直保持到20世纪70年代。随后又开始反弹。今天，贫富不均再次创下历史纪录，这可以帮助解释人们为什么重新对盖茨比现象产生了兴趣。菲茨杰拉德的小说最近被选为康奈尔大学和其他一些大学的普通读物，学校鼓励学生、教员、校友及其他工作人员阅读此书，对该书的讨论拉开了新学年的序幕。

encouraged to read and discuss the same book as the academic year begins.

With my last literature course, taken in high school, just a dim memory, I was naturally apprehensive when Cornell administrators asked me to speak at the university's Gatsby convocation① for incoming freshmen. In the process of preparing for that assignment, however, I was delighted to discover the extent to which my economics training actually seemed to illuminate important elements of the novel's story line. Consider, for example, the link between wealth and personal attractiveness. Everyone wants a home in a safe neighborhood with good schools, but those with low incomes cannot be sure of getting one. So economists are not surprised that women mention earning power at or near the top of the list when surveyed about traits they find attractive in men. Gatsby understood that his humble station in life made him an unlikely suitor for his coveted② Daisy. And so he labored with singular focus and determination to achieve material success on the grandest scale possible.

The theory of compensating wage differentials helps illuminate a particular detail of this quest. This theory holds that the more unpleasant and risky a job is, the more it pays. Some of the largest pay premiums, it turns out, are those paid to highly qualified people who are willing to do morally questionable work. Tobacco industry consultants, for example, were once paid extremely high fees for their willingness to testify under oath that smoking had not been shown to cause serious illnesses. Gatsby

① convocation [ˌkɔnvəˈkeiʃən] *n.* 召集；集会

② covet [ˈkʌvit] *v.* 垂涎，觊觎

隐约记得高中的最后一节文学课，康奈尔大学的负责人要我在为大学新生举行的"盖茨比"讨论会上发言，我的心惴惴不安。在准备的过程中，我欣喜地发现我的经济学培训课实际上反映了《了不起的盖茨比》中的一些重要思想。比如，对财富和个人魅力之间的联系的思索。每个人都想在有好学校的安全的街区里有个家，但是那些低收入的人就不能保证了。所以，当被调查男人的哪些特点有吸引力时，经济学家对女人把男人的赚钱能力放在第一位或比较靠前的位置并不感到惊讶。盖茨比意识到自己卑微的地位不可能使他成为他觊觎良久的黛茜的求婚者，他只有一个目标和决心，那就是尽可能在最大程度上获得物质的成功。

补偿性工资差异理论帮助解释了这个问题的一个特别的细节。一份越是令人厌恶、越是危险的工作，它的报酬就越高。大的保险理赔往往付给了那些愿意做具有道德疑问工作的高素质人员。比如，烟草公司的顾问曾经薪酬极高，因为他们愿意宣誓作证吸烟不会引起严重的疾病。盖茨比意识到要抓住一切机会实现目标，他就不能太小心拘谨。菲茨杰拉德没有透露盖茨比财富积累的细节。但是毫无疑问盖茨比的工作既不道德，也不合法。盖茨比当然也意识到如果他被抓住判刑，他的理想将成为泡影。但是不管怎样，如果走低风险的路，他可能已经失败了。

realized that to have any chance of achieving his goal, he could not be cautious or squeamish①. Fitzgerald never reveals the precise details of how Gatsby amassed his fortune. But he leaves little doubt that Gatsby's work was not just morally suspect, but also well outside the law. Gatsby surely realized that if he were caught and punished, his dream would evaporate. But no matter. A less risky path would have meant certain failure.

The burgeoning literature on the determinants of human well-being also sheds light on events in "Gatsby." Once the almost exclusive domain of psychologists, happiness studies began to attract the attention of economists after Richard A. Easterlin posed a timeless question in an influential 1974 paper, Does money buy happiness? Current research supports seemingly contradictory answers to this question. One is that in any given country, the average level of measured happiness remains essentially unchanged over time, even in the face of substantial growth in average incomes. But if getting more money does not make us happier, why do people often struggle so hard to earn more? An answer is suggested by other studies showing that at a single point in time, people are happier, on average, the more money they have. To the extent money influences measured happiness levels, then, it is relative, not absolute, income that seems to matter.

But since Gatsby's income was enormous, in both relative and absolute terms, why wasn't he happy? Researchers have identified other factors that affect happiness levels far more than income does. For example, happiness levels rise substantially with the number of close

---

① squeamish [ˈskwiːmiʃ] *adj.* 过分讲细节的，过于拘谨的

“盖茨比”指南

讨论决定财富因素的新兴文学可以解释“盖茨比”事件。当理查德·A.伊斯特林在1974年的一份有影响的报纸上提出“钱能买到幸福吗”这个永恒的话题之后，曾是心理学专属领域的幸福研究开始引起经济学家的关注，当前的研究似乎支持看似矛盾的答案。在任何既定的国家，可以用来衡量幸福的平均水平随着时间的推移，不会有显著变化，即使平均工资水平大幅上涨。但是如果挣很多钱不能让人更幸福，为什么还要那么拼命地去挣钱呢？其他的研究结果也给出了这个问题的答案，在一个单一的时间点，人们拥有的钱越多，就越幸福。在某种程度上，金钱影响了可衡量的幸福水平，而收入对幸福的影响是相对的，不是绝对的。

无论相对条件还是绝对条件，盖茨比都很有钱，他为什么不幸福？比如，幸福的水平随着好朋友的增多而显著提高。盖茨比的葬礼是小说中最令人感慨的场面之一：愿意出席的人寥寥无几。由于拼命追求物质上的成功，他几乎没有真正的朋友。盖茨比的不幸还可以这样理解，那些有意识地特别专注物质成功的人，享有较低的可衡量幸福水平。这个发现对于把赚钱定为唯一目标、25岁成为巨富的大学新生来说是一个重要的启示。

根据快乐文学的原则，比较英明的策略就是找你喜欢做的工作。那些发现这种理念的人通常将其深深地植根于他们的职业生

friends someone has. One of the most striking scenes in the novel is of Gatsby's funeral, which almost no one bothered to attend. In his single-minded pursuit of material success, he appears to have developed no real friendships at all. Gatsby's unhappiness may also be explained in part by the finding that those who focus most consciously and intensely on material success also tend to experience low levels of measured happiness. This is a singularly important finding for the many incoming freshmen whose only apparent goal is to become fabulously① wealthy by age 25.

A far more promising strategy, according to the happiness literature, is to seek work you love. Those who find such a calling typically become deeply engaged in their professional lives. And engagement, in turn, leads to expertise, which in some fields, at least, leads to wealth. Finding work that you value for its own sake is thus not only a promising path to happiness, it may also increase your chances of becoming rich. But even if not, it will improve your odds of becoming an interesting person, someone who is attractive to both friends and potential mates alike. F. Scott Fitzgerald probably would have appreciated the Zen-like quality of this finding. Although the novelist himself married a woman from a prosperous family, he advised others not to marry for money. "Go where the money is," he counseled, "then marry for love."

(929 words)

① fabulously [ˈfæbjuləsli] *adv.* 极其,非常

涯。 回过头来看，这种植入与你的专业密切相关，而这种专业在某些领域，至少会通向财富。 找到一个你真正珍惜的工作不仅是通向成功的光明大道，还会增加致富的机会。 即便两者都不是，它也能增加你成为对朋友、对未来的伴侣有吸引力的、有趣的人的机会。菲茨杰拉德可能也会欣赏这个发现的禅宗哲学。 尽管作者自己娶了富家女，他还是建议其他人不要为了金钱而结婚。“向着钱去，为爱结婚”，他如是说。

知识链接

The Great Gatsby 《了不起的盖茨比》出版于 1925 年，是美国作家佛兰西斯·史考特·菲茨杰拉德所写的一部以 20 世纪 20 年代的纽约市及长岛为背景的长篇小说。盖茨比经常在家举办大型豪华聚会，大宴宾客，以显示其阔绰，目的是为了吸引从前的恋人黛西并赢回她的芳心。在盖茨比去海外参加第一次世界大战期间，他曾经的恋人黛西由于利欲熏心嫁给了出身于富豪家庭的纨绔子弟汤·布坎南。然而物欲和肉欲的满足并没能填补黛西精神上的空虚与贫乏，她与盖茨比重逢后好像又旧情复燃。但黛西已不是原来的黛西，她不再是盖茨比想象中的纯情女孩，而是一个愚蠢、自私、庸俗、美丽的躯壳。后来黛西在一次酒后驾驶盖茨比的车时轧死了汤姆的情妇，却与汤姆一道密谋并残忍地嫁祸于盖茨比，导致死者的丈夫突然闯入盖茨比家中并开枪打死了盖茨比，然后自杀身亡，使盖茨比最终彻底成为自私而残忍的黛西的牺牲品。这部小说被视为美国文学“爵士时代”的象征。